Online Marketing Terms Exposed: Understand the Lingo of
Online Search Marketing Experts

By Gary E. Haffer

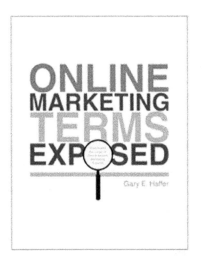

Online Marketing Terms Exposed: Understand the Lingo of
Online Search Marketing Experts

By Gary E. Haffer

Copyright © 2009

ISBN: 1-4392-2747-0
Library of Congress Control Number: 2009901363

Online Marketing Terms Exposed: Understand the Lingo of Online Search
Marketing Experts

BookSurge Publishing
7290-B Investment Dr
N. Charleston SC 29418
www.booksurge.com

Printed in the United States of America

*Online Marketing Terms Exposed,* is available at special quantity discounts for bulk
purchases, sales promotions, employee premiums, and educational use. Please
contact us for further information at www.booksurge.com or
onlinemarketingterms@gmail.com.

ISBN: 1-4392-2747-0

Library of Congress Number: 2009901363

## Dedication
I would like to dedicate this to my Dad.
For all the laughter we shared and the life lessons he taught me that have stayed with me all my life.

## About the Author
Gary E. Haffer is an online marketing expert, author, speaker, blogger, and a former director of the Apple User group of the Boston Computer Society, the first social networking group. For over nine years, he has been a trusted source for business marketing experience, from small businesses to Fortune 500 companies. Currently he leads the online marketing efforts of Boston Interactive.

## Author's Acknowledgement
Special thanks to Sara A. Praeger without her amazing talents this book would not be what it is today. She is an expert in her field.

Thanks go out to:

Chuck Murphy, CEO of Boston Interactive

John Francis, President of Boston Interactive

Dan Beadle and Matt Berube for their artistic eye and design.

To my family and friends.

# FORWARD

Some books do a great job of discussing the theoretical, they get you nodding your head and thinking "that's a great idea; I wonder how I can apply that to my business or area of responsibility." Gary E. Haffer does a nice job of answering this question for those of us who work within the Interactive Services business. By providing a very simple to understand and practical explanation of the multi-faceted SEO arena, he has created a useful "how-to" explanation for people new to the SEO market, while providing a comprehensive reference book for the more experienced audiences. Search Engine Marketing has become a progressively more important part of what all interactive professionals do, and this book can be an extremely useful component of your toolkit. Whether in building out new websites, enhancing the SEO performance of an existing website, or just trying to better understand how two seemingly similar websites can perform so differently from a search perspective, Gary has written a very practical book that I think you will find to be both easy to read and full of tips to implement.

Search Engine Optimization and Search Engine Marketing are not just tasks that are turned over to the SEO folks after a website is developed, or when a website isn't performing up to management's expectations; it should be a part of the very conception of every website effort.

From the definition and analysis of your target audience, your understanding of their decision making process and the way that they evaluate your offerings, it is important to understand your audience and their objectives. Gary Haffer's book helps you to understand some of the ways that you can take this information and, through very small changes to a website, have an incredible impact on the website's performance. I recommend that you buy this book, but more importantly, I recommend that you put in place SEO and SEM practices. They will add a great deal to your interactive communications efforts.

John Francis
President of Boston Interactive

# TABLE OF CONTENTS

# INTRODUCTION

I can't help remembering what it was like in 1992 when I was working at a high tech company. Sitting on my desk was a corded phone that had no voice mail, some paper clips, tape, White Out, and a tray for faxes. This wasn't the Middle Ages; although, it was a number of years ago. The receptionist took all the phone messages, wrote them down on pink slips, and left them in the labeled compartments of a circular plastic tray so we could pick them up at the end of the day. Any urgent messages were delivered to us within a few hours. Other than paper, pens, and pencils with erasers that's all that was on my desktop (called a table top at that time).

My day was still pretty busy. A small part of my day was consumed with reading client faxes, advertisement faxes for travel deals, or faxes from deposed leaders from parts of the world that I never knew about. These were the most interesting faxes because they promised to give me a million dollars if I would deposit their money into my savings account for them. All I needed to do was to fax them the name of my bank, account number, password, login name, date of birth, my address, and phone number. (I guess they didn't know how to get to America to open up a savings account because they were not US citizens).

Communications was even more of a problem. There was no Gmail, Google, Yahoo, Instant Messenger, text messages, call waiting, chat rooms, Facebook or anything else. If there was anything else available aside from my office phone, I didn't use it.

Talk about searching for products and services, the methods available were quite simple. They consisted of the Yellow Pages, White Pages, and bingo cards from magazines. I spent a great deal of time either on the phone with operator assistance or turning page after page of telephone books looking at ads trying to find something that suited my needs. I can still feel the frustration of finally finding the vendor I had been searching for, calling on the telephone, and discovering that they had gone out business or were too busy to talk to me. The phone books were updated once a year – so the information was seldom current. It felt good living in the information age.

Let's fast forward ten years, my desk has radically changed. I have a phone (still corded) that has voice mail, call transferring, call forwarding, and a computer that connects me to the Internet. I can use a scanner, email, Instant Messenger, Facebook.com, Twitter, and a browser that help me find almost anything I want with the help of search engines.

I find anything and everything in about 10 seconds and I am constantly searching for anything and everything. I haven't used a phone book in years, but I think that they still deliver them once a year. Oh, my Fax machine is still used for sending back signed business documents, but that is about all it does.

We are truly in an online world thanks to the Internet. Newspapers are online, and marketing brochures are readily available from websites as is real-time online customer support. Online marketing has completely changed our world with a progressively larger portion of advertising devoted to the website and search engine optimization. Another thing that is different and challenging for anyone to understand is the language of this online world.

The lingo of online marketing is unique to the online world. The language is a compilation of terms that are common expressions, technology slang, acronyms, and phrases that the Internet experts have invented. This lingo, whether borrowed from computer programmers and technicians or newly invented, can be confusing and is often akin to a foreign language in terms of conveying the real meaning of what is being communicated. To understand online marketing, you need to know these terms and their meaning.

## Why you should read this book

This book will present the language of the online world and a "*how-to*" course on how to do the common optimization tasks on and off the web, social media, and more.

If you want to:

- Know more about online marketing, SEO, Pay-per-Click, or Social Media
- Be able to understand Online Marketing consultants
- See if SEO is something you would like to pursue for a career
- Learn how search engines, SEO, Pay-per-Click, and Social Media can help a website
- Understand the techniques to make a website (or future website) search friendly
- Just want to try your hand at optimizing your own website or future website
- Or just for the fun of understanding online marketing jargon

If you fall into any of these categories, then I'm sure that you will enjoy this book and have no problem following its advice. Again, its primary focus is the language of online marketing and how a business person can understand these terms and put them into play on and off the web.

## Organization of this book

I wrote this book with the intention that anyone would be able to understand what is being discussed. Words that have special meanings are bold and italicized. For example,

> **_Search marketing_** is a process ...."

Here "**_search marketing_**" is in bold and italics. When you see a term like this, you can go into the glossary for a definition of that term.

Information that may be useful is denoted by **HINT:** in the text.

## Primary Topics Covered

The primary topics this book covers are:

- How search engines operate to deliver traffic
- Creating and using keyword phrases to describe a website focus
- Creating and implementing Meta Tags
- On-Site Optimization
- Off-Site Optimization
- Ways to attract traffic from social media and other sources
- Understanding Pay-per-Click
- Why press releases and the social media are important
- Techniques to avoid so that you don't get in trouble
- Gary's believe it or not about websites, Google and more

This book should be read sequential from cover to cover in order to understand all the concepts.

For those of you who are looking for specific topics, the table of contents is detailed enough to allow the picking and choosing of chapters.

## What I Understand About You

I have no preconceived notions about your technical skills other than a basic familiarity with PCs, how to surf the Internet, a general understanding of websites, and have used some form of email. It is not necessary to have a background in online marketing, SEO, Pay-per-Click, or Social Media.

## Reaching the Author

Gary E. Haffer can be reached by email at onlinemarketingterms@gmail.com or at his blog www.ghaf123.wordpress.com.


Thanks and enjoy my book.

CHAPTER 1:
# Understanding Search Engines

***Chapter Contents***
- Using Search Engines for results
- Why Search Engines are important
- Types of search optimization
- Pay-per-Click Search Optimization
- Organic Search Engine Optimization
- Comparing Pay-per-Click to Organic Search

Before the Internet, the main method of advertising consisted of newspaper, magazine, television, or radio advertisements. Because of the high costs of other media, small businesses used magazine advertisements to get inquiries and to make sales. Magazine advertisements required ads to be placed in publications several months in advance of their scheduled publication dates and the ads often didn't change for four to six months. If a particular ad failed to generate traffic, it usually took four months for the advertiser to realize it. The selling cycle was also long because it took at least a month to two months to receive inquiries from potential customers who had seen ads in magazines.

These inquiries were often from students or individuals who just wanted information and knew very little about the product or services being offered. Other inquiries just wanted to obtain literature and many were from other companies who were seeking information about their competitors. The inquiries which were generated from magazine ads were delivered to the advertiser via the United Post Office, the old way to mail information, in the form of "**bingo card**" leads; they acquired that name because **prospects** would check off numbers on postcards inside magazines to indicate what aspect of the product or service they were interested in. The "*bingo card*" leads then arrived at the advertiser's location about two weeks later. The "*bingo cards*" needed qualification with regard to valid phone numbers, street addresses, and zip codes before any contact could be made with the prospect. From the time a prospect filled out a "*bingo card*" to the time the company received and qualified the leads and began the sales process, three to six weeks could have passed. Prospects were lost strictly because of this long lead time.

## Using Search Engines for Results

Online marketing has become popular because it can be cost effective and produces almost instantaneous results. Now, individuals search on the Internet using search engines such as **Google**, **Yahoo**, **MSN**, and others and get results in a matter of seconds. They can look for products and service offerings 24/7 and qualify themselves as valuable prospects all by using a search engine.

Search engines are websites that gather information about websites, **web pages,** and documents.  They use technology to **crawl** through websites to obtain information about specific topics and then store that information in their **databases** (*index*). The majority of traffic to websites originates from the major search engines. Popular search engines include Google, Yahoo, and MSN. If a website cannot be found by the search engines, it has no opportunity to have its content **index**ed. This can be devastating to the online marketer because if a website's data is not in a search engine's database, that website will not be displayed in the results of a **query** and potential prospects will not be directed to that website.

## Why Search Engines are Important

Building a website, an online storefront that is open 24/7, is the first step in creating **traffic** and making sales. Next is the understanding of how **search engines** deliver results. The third step is optimizing a website so that search engine can deliver maximum results.

When **keyword phrases** are entered in a search engine query that search engine searches its database to see what matches that keyword phrase. As it searches its database for these keyword phrases, it filters the results according to its own **algorithm** and other factors so it only displays what its algorithm has calculated to be relevant. These listings are displayed in the **search engine results page** (**SERP**) with the most relevant matches in the top positions and the least relevant ones in the bottom positions. The display will show every entry that the search engine has in its database at that particular time. What exactly does a search engine do? They actually do three things.

1. Index web pages and make a copy of web pages. Search engines store all the **HTML** content on a web page in their **database**.

2. Retrieve all the matching documents **relevant** for what is searched.

3. Rank web page content. This consists of the process of a search engine looking at documents retrieved for a search

*query* and places them in relevant order according to its algorithm.

Everyone knows search engines are the way that things are found and research is done on the Internet. How search engines work and what a website needs to obtain maximum traffic and sales are often misunderstood. Specifically, new online marketers are often confused about how the search engines produce results for their product offerings or services. In basic terms, search engines look for **relevancy** – how marketers' products or services relate to what the search engines have stored internally under major categories. In order for **visitors** to find a particular website, search engines display results that have been previously stored in their databases. The keywords that describe the categories of products or services with high **positions** generate the most amount of traffic, while lower positions generate some or no traffic. Using online marketing, search engines can be made to deliver the maximum quality traffic to a website.

## Types of Search Optimization

There are two major types of searches – **Organic search** optimization or Pay per Click **optimization**. Both types of search optimization can bring prospects to a website but the way each works is very different.

1. **Organic Search Engine Optimization** or **SEO** is a process where there is no charge to have keyword phrases placed high in the search engines results page. **Paid Search campaigns**, commonly called Pay-per-Click, requires **bidding** for that same placement. Both search methods generate traffic but they differ in their methods and costs.

### 2. **Pay-per-Click Campaigns**

Pay-per-Click search engine campaigns require an advertiser to pay a pre bid amount in order to have their advertisement appear in the sponsored links section. The advertisement's specific position and page is determined mainly by an amount of money paid to the search engine.
Sponsored links (Pay-per-Click Ads) appear on the top of the organic listings and to the right side of those listing. When a company stops paying (bidding on the keyword phrase) their ads disappear from sight and then everything is over unless the company resumes paying.

When visitors don't click on those ads, there are no charges to the advertiser and no traffic arrives at the advertiser's website from that campaign. It is similar to buying gas for a car. Every day or week the price of gas can change. The car travels a given distance based on the amount of gas put into the tank. Stop buying gas and the car stops moving. That concept is clear. Pay-per-Click requires that an advertiser pays forever for the traffic.

## Organic Search Engine Optimization

Organic Search Engine Optimization is essentially free because it does not require payment for each visitor's click made to a website.  What is required is paying (in some cases) for a professional to set up the website, distribute *press releases*, set up the initial SEO and research the marketing campaign. In some cases, hiring a professional SEO expert to make sure that an established SEO campaign is generating the maximum amount of traffic is also necessary. Both techniques rely on given search engines (like Google, Yahoo, MSN, or others) as their foundation for generating traffic. See Table 1-1.

## Organic SEO verses Pay-per-Click

Table 1-1 Comparison of Organic SEO verses Pay-per-Click

| Factors | Organic SEO | Pay-per-Click |
|---|---|---|
| Keyword phrases required | Yes | Yes |
| Results time frame | After 6 months | within 24 hours |
| Search Engine indexing needed | Yes | No |
| Website content requires optimization | Yes | No |
| Need to perform extra linking and other activities off the website | Yes | No |
| Keyword phrases must be bid for results | No bidding required | Yes |
| Calculating ROI straight forward | No - additional software required | Yes |
| Limits can be set for daily or monthly spend | No | Yes |
| Specific geographical areas can be targeted | No | Yes |
| Results depend on spend | No | Yes |
| When the spend stops so do the results | No | Yes |
| Impressions dependent on keyword phrase cost | No | Yes |

It is apparent from the preceding table the way traffic is used to produce results is quite different depending on what type of search is employed.

Now that we have explained search engines and how they produce results, let's talk about a vital component of a search – the keyword phrase.

## CHAPTER 2:

# Creating Keyword Phrases

## *Chapter Contents*

- Keyword phrases must be relevant
- Finding the best keyword phrases
- Understanding search behavior
- Keyword phrase analysis
- Analyzing keyword competition
- Keyword Ranking Index (KRI)
- Making the right choice in keyword phrases

---

The key to getting traffic to a website is through the keyword phrases that searchers enter into search engines to locate products, services, etc. As long as there is an understanding of the keyword phrases that visitors enter to find particular products or services, techniques can be performed in online marketing to generating traffic.

Keyword phrases can consist of one, two, three, or more words together which a searcher might use to describe a product or service when *searching* online. Online marketing is the process that correctly anticipates keyword phrases used by searchers to maximize the possibility that these visitors will increase your website traffic. There is a lot more involved in the process, but let's first start by understanding how to choose keyword phrases which represent a company's offerings – better known as relevancy.

## Keyword Phrases Must be Relevant

The first condition for selecting a keyword phrase is determining if that keyword phrase is relevant to a company's product offering. For example, if a query is entered for "*milk*", the search engine then searches its internal database for the category "*milk*" and displays its results on the search engine's results page (SERP) in order from the most relevant to the least relevant. The most relevant result is referred to as position one and the least relevant can be in position 200 or higher. Having the keyword phrases **rank** past the third page of search engine results is deadly because it is unlikely that even the most determined searcher will continue to scroll past the third page of search results.

## Finding the Best Keyword Phrases

In order to select keyword phrases that draw **traffic** to a website, there are certain conditions that must be satisfied. These conditions are as follows.

1.  Relevancy to the company's products and/or services.

2.  Popularity of keyword phrases. They should have a reasonable number of searchers each month.

A company that sells "Personal computer hard drives" should not consider the keyword phrase "*personal storage*" if it only has a search volume of twenty searchers per month. If that keyword phrase achieves the top ranking, then the volume of website traffic is around 10% of the search volume or two visitors per month. Two visitors per month hardly make a noticeable difference in website traffic. Optimizing a keyword phrase whose search volume (**popularity**) is 40,000 searches per month and is in the top position, produces about 4,000 visitors to a website.

3.   High *Keyword Ranking Index* – (KRI). These are relevant keyword phrases that have the highest monthly searches and the least amount of competition.

Many times keyword phrases that are picked are relevant with good monthly search volumes but have an unbelievable amount of competition. There is so much competition for these keyword phrases, even when optimized, that they will not rank high enough on the search engine results page (first, second or third page) to produce enough website traffic because of the competition. Selecting the best keyword phrase using KRI will be discussed.

## Understanding Search Behavior

Driving maximum website traffic involves understanding the keyword phrases the *target audience* uses to search for products and services often. Searchers describe what they are searching for using keyword phrases than are different from those one might commonly use of to describe a particular products or services.

For example, one searcher searching for running shoes might enter the keyword phrase "*running shoes*" and another searcher might enter the search term "*running sneakers.*" Both keyword phrases are valid search keyword phrases for running shoes but optimizing a website for one keyword phrase and not the other may result in missing a considerable amount of website traffic. This can be especially true if the monthly search volume for "running shoes" is 1,500 searchers per month, while "*running sneakers*" generates 90,000 searchers. That's where a keyword phrase analysis can help.

> **HINT:** The plural of a keyword phrase usually produces more searches per month than the singular version.

Here is a process to follow to generate the best keyword phrases.

1. Compile a preliminary list of all keyword phrases that will be used to search for particular products or services. Brainstorm with coworkers, friends, and acquaintances to create keyword phrases that are relevant to the company's offerings. Keyword phrases can be comprised of two, three, four or more words.

2. Look at competitors' websites for their keyword phrases. In order to accomplish this task, type their **URL** into the address bar on a computer's **browser**. Now enter the **view source code** on your browser. Look at the **Meta Tags** on the competitors' website for keyword phrases, **Meta Title tags**, and **Meta Description tags**. This will also provide a starting point for the next step.

3. Once the preliminary list has been generated, use **Google AdWords Keyword Tool** to obtain the monthly search volume for that keyword phrase.

The URL for Google AdWords™ Keyword Tool is: (https://adwords.google.com/select/keywordToolExternal).

To use Google AdWords™ Keyword Tool (GAKT), enter the URL. Once the website appears on the screen, check off the box with the special characters to proceed. GAKT will suggest keyword phrases relative to that website. By combining the brainstorming words, competitor website keyword phrases, and the keyword phrase suggestions from Google AdWords Keyword Tool, there will be quite a few keyword phrases to analyze.

> **HINT:** The next part of the *keyword phrase* discovery process involves some math. It may be best to create an Excel spreadsheet to handle the mathematical calculations involved.

To facilitate the selection of keyword phrases refer to the sample website. See Figure 2.1.

Figure 2.1 Evan's Shoes Website

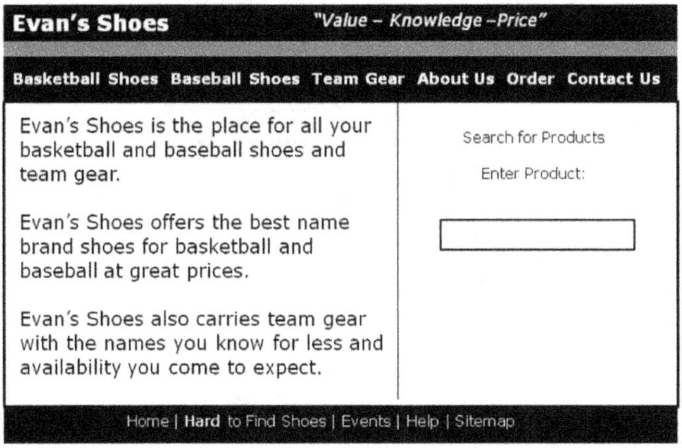

Let's start the discovery process by considering what types of visitors come to the Evan's Shoes website. Two important questions to ask about the visitors are:

Why are they coming to Evan's Shoes website?

What keyword phrases do they use to find Evan's Shoes?

## Keyword Phrase Analysis

Evan's Shoes sells basketball shoes, baseball shoes, and team gear only for men at big discounts.

By brainstorming, using Google AdWords™ Keyword tools, and looking at the competition, a preliminary list of five keyword phrases has been created. See Table 2-1.

Table 2-1 Preliminary list of sample keyword phrases for Evan's Shoes

| Keyword Phrases |
| --- |
| basketball shoes |
| buy basketball shoes |
| cheap basketball shoes |
| discount basketball shoes |
| men's basketball shoes |

This list represents the first pass of generating keyword phrases for Evan's Shoes website. At this point, the primary concern is making the keyword phrases relevant to the products and services offered.

The goal is to obtain as many relevant keyword phrases as possible in order to maximize website traffic. If the keyword is not relevant, toss it and replace it with others that are. This rule is demonstrated in Table 2-2.

Table 2-2 Rule of keyword phrase relevancy

| Keyword Phrase | Relevant to Company's Offerings | Action |
|---|---|---|
| basketball shoes | Yes | Continue keyword discovery |
| baseball shoes | Yes | Continue keyword discovery |
| basketball nets | No | Don't use |

The next phase of generating the right keyword phrases is to find the monthly *search volume*.

To calculate the search volume, continue to use the **Google AdWords™ Discovery Tool**.

**Google's AdWords™ Keyword Discovery Tool** (https://adwords.google.com/select/KeywordToolExternal) is easy to use and free. It displays the number of searches conducted for any given keyword phrase in the current month and the average monthly volume during the current year. This is an important number to capture because some keyword phrases may be seasonal and the number of searchers may fluctuate throughout the year.

**HINT:** For calculation of monthly searches for keyword phrases use the average monthly search numbers because they take into account monthly variations.

Let's look up four of the keyword phrases from our list. They are baseball shoes, baseball shoe, basketball shoe, and basketball shoes.  Evan's Shoes website sells basketball shoes and baseball shoes and so these keyword phrases seem like perfect choices. Choosing the plural seems more natural because searchers would search for shoes rather than a "*pair of basketball shoe*" We'll soon see how this works out.

Enter these keyword phrases into the GAKDT search box. After all the keyword phrases are entered, enter the visible code on the screen and press the submit button.

**HINT:** When keyword phrases are entered into the GAKT, many additional keyword phrases are also displayed. This is an added bonus because sometimes these additional keyword phrases are good matches to include.

Figure 2.2 displays the keyword phrases, and the average monthly search volumes.

Figure 2-2 Keyword phrases average monthly search volume

| ▲Keywords | Advertiser Competition ? | Local Search Volume: April ? | Global Monthly Search Volume ? |
|---|---|---|---|
| Keywords related to term(s) entered - sort by relevance ? | | | |
| basketball shoes | | 673,000 | 673,000 |
| buy basketball shoes | | 2,400 | 2,400 |
| cheap basketball shoes | | 14,800 | 14,800 |
| discount basketball shoes | | 4,400 | 3,600 |
| men's basketball shoes | | 22,200 | 40,500 |

Remember the Excel spreadsheet? Let's enter some fictitious data for some keyword phrases generated from the Evan's

Shoes website into the spreadsheet so that more calculations can be performed.

Our spreadsheet should resemble that of Table 2-3.

Table 2-3. Keyword phrases and monthly search volume

| Keyword Phrases | Monthly Search Volume |
|---|---|
| basketball shoes | 673,000 |
| buy baseball shoes | 2,400 |
| cheap basketball shoes | 14,800 |
| discount basketball shoes | 3,600 |
| men's basketball shoes | 40,500 |

**HINT**: A rule of thumb is to choose keyword phrases that have a minimum search volume of 1,500 searches a month. Keyword phrases that attain the first position on page one of the search engine results will only contribute around 10% of their search volume visitors to the website. (Other positions produce less traffic) Choosing a keyword phrase with only 200 visitors searching for that keyword phrase can only deliver 20 visitors per month maximum. Not enough traffic to make a difference.

Higher search volumes data is not the only factor to consider. The amount of competition for that keyword phrase has to be factored in. To calculate the competition for that keyword phrase proceed as follows:

- Record the monthly search volume for the initial keyword phrases list. Now create a column for annual searches.

- To create annual searches multiply the monthly searches by 12 for each monthly search number.

> The **Keyword Ranking Index (KRI)** is based on annual numbers and is calculated in annual terms.

At this point the Excel spreadsheet of fictitious data for Evan's Shoes website should resemble Table 2-4.

Table 2-4 Monthly/annual search volume of keyword phrases

| Keyword Phrases | Monthly Search Volume | Annual Search Volume |
|---|---|---|
| basketball shoes | 673,000 | 8,076,000 |
| buy baseball shoes | 2,400 | 28,800 |
| cheap basketball shoes | 14,800 | 177,600 |
| discount basketball shoes | 3,600 | 43,200 |
| men's basketball shoes | 40,500 | 486,000 |

Let's recap the data.

Right now there are no keyword phrases that are less than 1,500 searches per month. So, there are no keyword phrases to exclude.

Although all of the other five keyword phrases seem attractive, it is unwise to be too hasty in selecting them.  Although there are a lot of searches each month, taken into account the competition for that keyword phrase. This is necessary in order to obtain all the relevant keyword phrases with the most volume and the least amount of competition. Let's see how to calculate the competition for these phrases.

## Analyzing Keyword Competition

To analyze the competition, use the **Google™ search engine** itself (*www*).

Type the URL *www* and hit Enter. When the **query box** appears, type "*basketball shoes*" just as it appears here, that is, within quotation marks.

HINT: *Exact match* is a more accurate way to get the competition because  a searcher must enter all the terms in the exact order rather than only entering a random word into a search engine like "*basketball*".

Enter keyword phrases enclosed in quotes one at a time and record the competition. Figure 2-3 displays the Google Search engine results for the competition for the keyword phrase "*basketball shoes.*"

At the top of the Google search engine results page is a number stating that Results 1 -10 of about 2,700,000 websites are competing for the keyword phrase "*basketball shoes*". The

2,700,000 is the number to use for the competition. See Figure
2-3.

---

Figure 2-3 Competition for basketball shoes on Google

---

Continue entering the keyword phrases, one at a time and
record that number in the Excel spreadsheet until all the
keyword phrases are entered. A sample Excel spreadsheet for
Evan's Shoes is displayed in Table 2-5.

---

Table 2-5   Keyword phrases, search volume and competition

---

| Keyword Phrase | Monthly Search Volume | Annual Search Volume | Number of Competitors for keyword phrase |
|---|---|---|---|
| basketball shoes | 673,000 | 8,076,000 | 2,700,000 |
| buy baseball shoes | 2,400 | 28,800 | 21,400 |
| cheap basketball shoes | 14,800 | 177,600 | 23,000 |
| discount basketball shoes | 3,600 | 43,200 | 6,240 |
| men's basketball shoes | 40,500 | 486,000 | 65,400 |

## The Keyword Ranking Index

At this point the keyword phrases with the *highest searches*
and the lowest amount of competition need to be identified.
This is what is referred to as the Keyword Ranking Index or
KRI.

To calculate KRI add another column for the KRI data in the spreadsheet and perform the calculation shown in Figure 2-3.

This success factor column called Google KRI is:

---

Figure 2-3. Calculating KRI for each keyword phrase

---

> KRI for keyword phrase on Google = Annual Search Volume /
> Number of Competitors for this Keyword Phrase

See Table 2-6 for a sample spreadsheet.

---

Table 2-6 Keyword phrases with Keyword Ranking Index

---

| Keyword Phrase | Monthly Search Volume | Annual Search Volume | Number of Competitors for keyword phrase | Google KRI |
|---|---|---|---|---|
| basketball shoes | 673,000 | 8,076,000 | 2,700,000 | 2.99 |
| buy baseball shoes | 2,400 | 28,800 | 21,400 | 1.35 |
| cheap basketball shoes | 14,800 | 177,600 | 23,000 | 7.72 |
| discount basketball shoes | 3,600 | 43,200 | 6,240 | 6.92 |
| men's basketball shoes | 40,500 | 486,000 | 65,400 | 7.43 |

The entry under Google KRI (because it only pertains to searches on the Google search engine) can be a number or a fraction. This is an important number because it represents the odds of having this keyword phrase ranked on the first three pages (positions 1 through 30) of a Google search results page.

---

**HINT:** The first three positions on Google are the only positions that generate traffic.

---

## Making the Right Choice

This is where the rubber hits the road. The rule states that KRIs less than 0.15 should be tossed out right away because these keyword phrases after optimization will never be able to rank in the first three pages on a Google search engine.

Are there any keyword phrases that will not work? No. They all have a KRI over .15 so these will work out well.

Keyword phrases like "*basketball shoes*" and "cheap *basketball shoes*" are the best bets to really rank high once optimized.

A sample of the final keyword phrases chosen to be used for Evan's Shoes website is displayed in Table 2-7.

Table 2-7 Sample of the final keyword phrases for Evan's Shoes

| Keyword Phrase | Monthly Search Volume | Annual Search Volume | Number of Competitors for keyword phrase | Google KRI |
|---|---|---|---|---|
| basketball shoes | 673,000 | 8,076,000 | 2,700,000 | 2.99 |
| buy baseball shoes | 2,400 | 28,800 | 21,400 | 1.35 |
| cheap basketball shoes | 14,800 | 177,600 | 23,000 | 7.72 |
| discount basketball shoes | 3,600 | 43,200 | 6,240 | 6.92 |
| men's basketball shoes | 40,500 | 486,000 | 65,400 | 7.43 |

This is just a sample of the keyword phrases that can be used for Evan's Shoes website. The keyword list should be around twenty to thirty keyword phrases for the best traffic.

Now that a keyword phrases list has been generated, let's proceed to the next vital component of search optimization - creating Meta Tag.

CHAPTER 3:

# Using Meta Tags

**Chapter Contents**
- Meta Title Tag
- Meta Description Tag
- Meta Keyword Tag
- Alt Tag

Now that keyword phrases have been created, they can be used to build Meta tags, Alt tags, and **header tags** on the web pages. This chapter demonstrates how to create and place the keyword phrases on the web pages with Meta tags and the like. Let's start with an important one – the Meta Title tag.

## Meta Title Tag

The Meta Title Tag is an important piece of information for Google and other search engines. It conveys to the search engine the focus or main topic of each web page so that the page can be properly categorized and indexed. A Meta Title tag should be relevant to the products and/or services being offered on the website.

Meta Title tags, which are lines of HTML code, are always placed near the top of the HTML code for each web page. Meta Title tags are visible to the visitor in the search engine's results page (SERP) and also appear in the browser when a visitor looks at a web page.

> **HINT:** Try to use one or two relevant keyword phrases in a Meta Title tag for each web page. This will help a search engine place that web page in the proper category of its database.

Creating a Meta Title tag is quite simple. Here is how it works:

1. Write an accurate summary description of the web page. The Meta Title tag can be up to 70 characters (including spaces) in length and the first letter of each keyword phrase should be capitalized.

> **HINT:** A good way to start is to jot down the URL of the individual web page and then the focus of the page.

2. Format the Meta Title tags by separating the main terms from one another with any one of these symbols (|), (-), (>), (.), (,) or a combination of them. The vertical bar or **stove pipe** between the web page title and the keyword phrases is best because it more clearly separates the information.

Let's create Meta Title Tags for Evan's Shoes Home Page (a fictitious website) that sells basketball shoes, baseball shoes, and team gear. Here is where the optimal keyword phrases are used.

Here are some examples of Meta Title Tags for Evan's Shoes website:

> *Evan's Shoes – We sell Basketball Shoes, Baseball Shoes, and Team Gear*

Or

> *Evan's Shoes | Basketball Shoes| Baseball Shoes| Team Gear*

Or

> *Evan's Shoes > Basketball Shoes| Baseball Shoes| Team Gear*

*Evan's Shoes* is the Home Page and three keyword phrases used in the Meta Title tag are *basketball shoes, baseball shoes,* and *team gear.*

## Best Practices for Meta Title Tags:

1. Meta title tags should be different for every web page because every web page is focused on a different topic.

2. Always include one or two keyword phrases.

3. Punctuation can be used to separate keyword phrases or ideas in the tag. Minimize the use of common words such as and, the, of, and in. They are not recognized by the search engines.

4. Meta title tags should be accurate and short. There are no penalties for having a Meta Title tag only 30 characters in length.

5. Meta title tags should be the focus or main topic of the web page.

Placing a Meta Title Tag on a web page is simple. Here's how it works:

1.  Access a website or request assistance from the **webmaster** . Once the web page has been accessed, enter the following HTML code after the <Head> marker located at the top of the web page.

2.  <title> *Evan's Shoes - Basketball Shoes and Team Gear at the lowest prices*</title>

**Avoid the following:**

*   Leaving a Meta Title Tag as "Home Page", "Title Page" or "Evan's Shoes".

*   Having duplicate *Meta Title Tags* for each web page.

*   Making a Meta Title Tag so general that the search engines can't figure out what the tag means.

# Meta Description Tag

The Meta Description Tag is also an important piece of information for Google and other search engines. It provides a summary of the web page. The Meta Description Tag is displayed on the search engine's results page (SERP). Since it may direct potential visitors to the web page, it must be to the point and relevant so that a potential searcher can determine that this is the desired the web page.

The length of a Meta Description Tag is 150 spaces. This includes characters and blank spaces. Any characters beyond 150 are not displayed on the search engine's result page. This looks bad if partial words appear.

Creating a Meta Description tag is quite simple. Here is how it works:

1.  Write a brief description of the web page. Make it descriptive enough so that a visitor can tell just by glancing at this page that it matches the *search criteria*. Make sure to keep the length under 150 characters (including spaces) and to capitalize the first letter of each keyword phrase.

> **HINT:** A good way to start is to jot down what a potential visitor to should know about this web page in 150 characters or less.

2.  Meta Description tags are not the same as Meta Title tags in that they are 150 character descriptions or summaries of a page. As such, they are not quite as rigid but they should be made to stand out in a search engine's results page (SERP).

3.  Always add one or two keyword phrases in the Meta Description tag. Remember to capitalize the first letter of each keyword phrases.

4.  Let's create a Meta Description Tag for Evan's Shoes Home Page that sells basketball shoes, baseball shoes, and team gear.

Here are examples for a Meta Description Tag for Evan's Shoes Home Page:

> Evan's Shoes offers a wide variety of Basketball Shoes, Baseball Shoes, and Team Gear at the best prices and availability.

Place the Meta Description tag within the <head> page of the HTML code for that web page. Add the HTML to the tag so that it is in the following format:

```
<meta name="description" content="Evan's Shoes offers a wide variety of Basketball Shoes, Baseball Shoes, and Team Gear at the best prices and availability"/>
```

The Meta Description Tag appears in a search engine results page, as follows:

**Evan's Shoes** offers a wide variety of **Basketball Shoes**, **Baseball Shoes**, and **Team Gear** at the best prices and availability.

Words displayed in bold indicate that they are relevant keyword phrases on this web page.

### Best Practices for Meta Description Tags:

1.  Make them unique for every web page.

2.  They should be no longer than 150 characters including spaces.

3.  Include one or two keyword phrases.

4.  Include a Meta Description tag for each web page.

5.  Make them an accurate summary of the web page.  Make the description as concise as possible. There are no penalties for having a Meta Description tag only 90 characters in length.

6.  Make them meaningful. Meta Description tags like "*Evan's Website*", "*Description Page*", "*This is a web page*", or "*Gary's Shoes Main web page*" do nothing to help the search engines to catalog the page or to guide visitors to the page.

# Meta Keyword Tag

The **Meta Keyword Tag** in the past was used to obtain a better page ranking for specific keyword phrases.  Today it is largely ignored by most search engines because they no longer place any significance. To use Meta Keyword Tags on a web page (to increase keyword density), only use a maximum of 10 keyword phrases so as not to cause keyword phrase overstuffing and or trouble with some search engines.

---

**HINT:** There is no loss in ranking if the Meta Keyword Tags are avoided.

## Alt Tags

Using images on a website is very popular and looks great but there is a downside. Search engines can't read images or other types of *flash* unless a piece of HTML code is placed in the code. This code or tag is referred to as an *Alt tag*. It is a short description that usually contains two to three keyword phrases about the image, or more. The Alt tag allows text to be specified for the image that otherwise search engines, visitors with browsers that don't support images, or special types of readers would leave as unknown.

> **HINT:** To tell if an image on a web page has an Alt tag associated with it, move the mouse over the image. If a small amount of text appears, the image has an Alt tag associated with it otherwise it needs one.

For example, an effective Alt tag and format describing an image of Evan's 1985 old basketball shoes worn in a tournament game looks as follows:

<img src=http://www.evanshoes.com/img/1985-evanshoes.jpg alt="Evan's 1985 basketball sneakers"/>

The image file's name is "*1985-evanshoes.jpg.*" It is named this way because this name makes the file easy to locate and is descriptive of its **content.** The search engines know how to classify the image and would do so under "*Evan's 1985 basketball sneakers.*"

## Best practices for Alt tags:

1.  Include a keyword phrase or two in the Alt tag for every image.

2.  Make Alt tags no longer than four words.

3.  Always include an Alt tag for *each image.*

4.  Make each Alt tag unique for each image.

The following Alt tags show how keyword phrases are used to increase the value to search engines.

For example, a file name of "Evansbasketballshoes.jpg" has the keyword phrase *basketball shoes* in the file name and it is a keyword phrase as well.

> **HINT:** As always, try to use images sparingly. They take up space and may slow down website load time.

In the next chapter, optimization of the website will be discussed. This is referred to as **On-Site optimization** or **On-Site SEO**.

CHAPTER **4**:

# Optimizing On-Site

*Chapter Contents*
- Anchor Tags
- Robot Tag
- Header Tags
- URL Structure
- Website Content

With Meta Tags in place, additional tags, URL structure, and website content need to be added. Let's start with the first element – The *Anchor Tag*.

## Anchor Tags

Anchor tags contain text that is associated with links. This text is easily readable by the search engines and makes it easier to allow those links to be indexed. Anchor tags should contain relevant keyword phrases like the Meta Tags.

It is simple to create Anchor Tags, let's again refer to the website - Evan's Shoes. Here is an example:

> *Evan's Shoes sell the best athletic shoes on the market at prices you can't beat.*
>
> *You can learn more about the <u>basketball shoes</u> we carry by selecting the Basketball button.*

Basketball shoes are the text in the link to a web page about basketball shoes and the code associated with it contains an anchor tag. The anchor tag's HTML code associated with that link may resemble something like:

> *You can learn more about the basketball shoes we carry*
> *at* `<a href="basketball-shoes.html"> Basketball`
> `Shoes</a>`

---

**HINT:** Always make the text in an anchor relative to the focus of destination web page. For example, never make an anchor tag called *basketball shoes* land on a web page about *team gear*.

---

### Best practice for Anchor Tags:

1. Include a keyword phrase in the Anchor Tag text link.

2. Anchor tags that consist of more than a single word should include dashes to separate the words.

3. Never create an Anchor tag without using a keyword phase.

4. Make the Anchor tag unique for each phrase. For example, *Basketballs* should have a different Anchor tag than *Basketball Shoes*.

## Robots Tag

The robot tag is reserved exclusively for *search engine spiders*. This tag instructs spiders to index a specific web page and follow all links on that web page or ignore the web page and its links.

If there is any doubt about spiders following all links and indexing web pages, then this HTML code should be added to all web pages as the default setting. The Robot tag for INDEX and Follow in HTML is below:

```
<META name ="robots" content="index, follow">
```

On the other hand, the *No Follow command* prohibits bad comments on a web page to be indexed. This is useful for websites  that accept public comments from visitors or sources with doubtful reputation or susceptible to **SPAM**. The NOFOLLOW command stops search engines from doing anything with that web page.

The Meta robot tag for NOINDEX and NOFOLLOW in HTML code format is below:

```
<META name ="robots" content="noindex, nofollow">
```

When a Robot tag is used, it should be placed in the same *directory* as the Home Page.

## Header Tags

Header tags not only style the text that appears on a web page but also indicate headings for the various sections of a web page's text. The Header Tags purpose is to help the search engines understand what is important about a web page's content. (Basically enforces a Meta Title Tag)

> **HINT:** Place at least one keyword phrase in a header tag.

An H1 Header tag is the most important header tag that can be placed on a web page because it have a large font and search engines have been set up to pay special attention to a H1 tags.

> **HINT:** After H1 and H2 header tags, the rest of the header tags are not as important and the search engine spiders give H3 – H5 tags some attention, but not much.

Header tags can appear anywhere within the main code body of the HTML code of a web page. The format of a H1 Header tag is:

<h1> Text</h1>

Replace the text area with *Evan's Shoes has the best prices on Basketball shoes* on Evan's Shoes website. The H1 header tag code then becomes:

<h1>Evan's Shoes has the best prices on Basketball Shoes</h1>

> **HINT:** Header tags should always include at least one keyword phrase.

## URL Structure

URL's on a website should be easy for a search engine and a human to understand. The URL is important to the visitor as well as the search engine and it is displayed when a search engine displays the results of a query. All relevant words in a query will be highlighted in the search engine results page (SERP).

Here is an example of a confusing URL. It is confusing because of the many numbers and lack of description in the address. The bad URL is:

> *http://www.evanshoes.com/folder2/61748412l2/x1/044a.htm*

Since visitors like to use links to get to a website, creating a URL like the one below, with a description phrase, may make it easier for a visitor to type in or link to a website.

> *http://www.evanshoes.com/basketball-Shoes*

### Best practice for URLs:

1. Include keyword phrases in an URL. If the URL matches the keyword phrase used by a searcher, there is a better chance that the search will be relevant.

2. Use dashes for URLs and avoid the "_"underscore. There has recently been a debate that the underscore in a URL

causes problems because the underscore is hard for search engines to index. Stick to the dashes if possible.

3. Never mix the *www and non www* versions of URL within the website. It is best to use the www version for all links and URLs on a website.

4. Always use lower case characters in a URL because they are easy to remember.

5. The URL, www.evanshoes.com can be treated by Google as different from evanshoes.com. So set up a **301 redirect** to ensure that the www version is your preferred version. At that point, make sure that all URLs on the website start with www to be consistent.

## Website Content

A website acts as a 24/7 storefront. A website should make it easy for visitors to find certain products and offerings. Using the techniques for keyword phrases that were developed earlier (Chapter 2) will help attract visitors searching for products or services offered. Once they have arrived at the website, its website content should convince them to make a purchase.

The content on a website should be targeted to a potential visitor's interest. One way to understand a visitor is to create a **persona**. The persona provides information about the visitors which in turn helps to determine keyword phrases and website content that a visitor might use to describe a particular product or service. It is basically a matter of profiling a visitor and identifying the criteria that will convince a visitor to make a purchase.

Content that informs and directs visitors to wanting more is the best type of content. The content should be fresh and compelling and scattered with keyword phrases.

## Best Practices for Website Content:

1. Always include keyword phrases on website or web page content.

2. Check the spelling of words and avoid slang terms.

3. Organize your headings into logical blocks.

4. Use language (reading level) that is targeted to your target audience and that they can understand.

5. Use dashes (-) and the slash (/) for **directories** but avoid the (_) underscore because the underscore is hard for search engines to index.

6. Never mix the www and non www *versions of URL* in your website. Always use the www version for all links and URLs.

7. Always use lower case URLs because people can remember them easier.

> **HINT:** Selling tee shirts to high school and college students may not be too effective if the website content is at the Graduate College level.

The next chapter discusses techniques to make a website search friendly. Website search friendly techniques include 404 custom error pages, **Google™** *Sitelinks*, and *favicons*.

CHAPTER 5:

# Making Search Engine Friendly Websites

## Chapter Contents

- Crawling every link without mistakes
- Retaining visitors and avoid unwanted exits
- Establishing a visual element for brand identity
- Google Sitelinks – visitor shortcuts
- Moving a website or web page

The basics are done. It's time to make a website friendlier to visitors. This chapter examines some essential items that should be included in every good website. This chapter discusses:

1. **XML Sitemaps** - a way for the search engine spiders to follow *links* to index websites and web pages.

2. Google Site Links (not always available for all websites) - a way to create and enter category links into search engine results (SERP)

3. Favicons - a small icon that can be bookmarked and used for brand identity.

4. Custom 404 Error Pages – this is a custom 404 error page, created for the website, that visitors lands on when they incorrectly enter an address that does not exist on the website or enter a misspelled URL.

5. *301 Redirects* – code that is used to redirect visitors away
   from a nonexistent page, link from a website URL that does
   not start with a www, or to a new web page from an old
   page.

## Crawling every link without mistakes

An **XML Sitemap** is a file that contains all the links in a
particular website. XML sitemaps help search engine spiders
navigate through the website without missing any link. Google
also uses an XML sitemap for building Google Sitelinks to add
additional links to particular listing when they are displayed in
the search engine results page.

Creating an XML Sitemap is really simple. There are many
sitemap tools on the market that will help to accomplish this
task and most of these tools are free. An online search for free
xml sitemap generators will yield many options, including the
**Google Sitemap generator**.

---

**HINT:** For other free tools for generating an XML sitemap
enter into a search query, "free xml sitemap generator." A
favorite is the Google sitemap generator.  Its URL is: (*www*).

---

2. Once a XML sitemap is generated either place it in the **root
directory** (ask for IT help if this task is too difficult for you) or
place it in another directory and note its location.

For example, here is the HTML code for the format of a site map for Evan's shoes.

*<sitemap_http://evanshoes/sitemap.xml>*

The sitemap will be used so that search engines can index every link on the website and optionally for Google Sitelinks.

> **HINT:** It is totally under Google's discretion to determine if Google Sitelinks will be helpful to a website and to allow them appear for a listing in the search engine results page.

## Retaining Visitors and Avoid Unwanted Exits

When visitors enter an URL address that does not exist, or has moved, or is incorrect, they receive a ***404 error*** (Page Not Found). Their next step would probably be to click on the back button and enter another URL on the website or go to another website. For example, a 404 Not Found error is generated if the following is entered with the word ordering misspelled.

*"www.evanshoes.com/orderring."*

A custom 404 error page may prevent visitors from leaving the website and help them find the information they want by providing helpful links.

The first step in creating a custom 404 error page is to request the webmaster or ***hosting company*** to enable the customization of this feature page for a website.

Here are a few guidelines to create a custom 404 error page.

1. Display possible alternative links. Common links are Contact Us, About, Products/Services, or a search field.

2. Include interesting visual elements to keep visitors engaged and avoid unwanted exits.

3. Include the home page address in a link on the page.

4. Remember to provide additional links to aid navigation.

5. Be user friendly – don't provide too many or too few links.

Let's take a look at a sample custom 404 error page. See Figure 5-1.

Figure 5-1    A Custom 404 Error Page

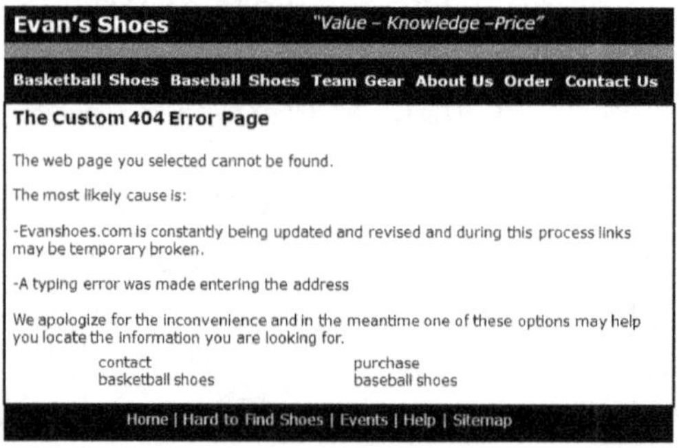

# Establishing a visual element for brand identity

A favicon is a 16 x 16 *pixel* that appears in the far left corner of the browser address bar.

The purpose of a favicon (favorite icon) is to establish a visual element for **brand identity** that visitors will always see. Favicons should be placed into a website's home directory under the <head> section of the Home Page.

In Figure 5-2 the favicon is the image of a basketball which appears to the left of the Meta Title tag in the browser window.

Figure 5-2 Example of a Favicon

## Best Practice for a Favicon:

1. Use an image that represents a product or service offered by your company.

HINT: Use only one favicon per website.

## Google™ Sitelinks – visitor shortcuts

Google Sitelinks are shortcuts that provide additional *navigation* for potential visitors. These links appear below the search engine results listing.

> **HINT:** As mentioned previous, Google decides which listings can benefit from Google Sitelinks and only allows those websites to use them.

An example of a Google Sitelinks listing (Contact, Purchase, Baseball shoes, and Store Locations are the Sitelinks) is displayed in Figure 5-3.

Figure 5-3 Example of Google  Sitelinks

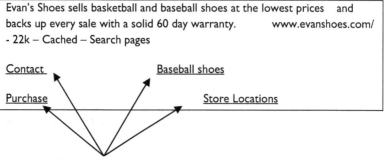

Evan's Shoes sells basketball and baseball shoes at the lowest prices    and backs up every sale with a solid 60 day warranty.          www.evanshoes.com/ - 22k – Cached – Search pages

Contact                        Baseball shoes

Purchase                            Store Locations

Using Google™ Sitelinks in an organic listing is simple. The steps are as follows:

1.  First, verify that an XML Sitemap exists on the web page. If a sitemap does not exist, then create one.

2. Go to **Google Webmaster Tools** and select Google Sitelinks.

3. In the Google webmaster tool, select the Sitelink column. Hopefully, links with an option to block or unblock them will appear. To block a link, just enter a check in the corresponding box. It's that simple.

## Moving a website or web page

Use a 301 redirect command to automatically redirect previously changed, updated, or deleted URLs to another URL. Let's look at redirecting *evanshoes.com* to *www.evanshoes.com*. Just enter the following into the home page HTML code for the redirect and you are done

The command is:

```
Redirect 301/evanshoes.com/file.html
http://www.evanshoes.com/directory/file.html
```

The first part of the command tells the search engine where the web page is currently residing and the last part tells it where to go.

### Best Practices for 301 Redirects

1. Use a 301 redirect to redirect website.com  to www.website.com.

2. Redirects can be used to redirect pages that are no longer in a *sitemap*. Using a 301 redirect prevents visitors from seeing a Page Not Found and they can be redirected to a working page without losing any visitor.

The next chapter discusses techniques to continue with the optimization of the *website*. These techniques are referred to as *Off-Site SEO*.  These techniques unlike the ones used on the website or web page, offer very little control of their results.

## CHAPTER 6:

# Off-Site SEO

*Topics Covered:*

- Submitting website info to directories
- Submitting articles to directories
- Online press releases
- Blogs – Word of Mouse
- Forums- Places to Contribute
- Getting results with Social bookmarking
- StumbleUpon.com
- Promoting a website offline

Now it's time to move off the website and start optimizing other areas. This type of optimization away from the website is called **Off-Site Optimization.**

Off-Site Optimization is still part of Search Engine Optimization but it requires a little more work. It involves constantly looking for places to mention a website and the keyword phrases associated with it so that the website can be "*picked up*" by other search engines and other sources. Let's take a look to see how Off-Site optimization works.

## Submitting website info to directories

The major benefit of submitting a website to a **directory** is to create links back to that website. The key to maximizing traffic and links is listing the website's information in all directories where visitors look for information.

There are two types of listing directories: free and paid directories.

## Best Practices for Submitting to Directories

Before submitting a particular website's information to directories, it is important to consider which directories are best suited to that company. Here are some simple guidelines to choosing the best directory.

1.  Choose directories that have a page rank of 3 or higher and high traffic.

2.  Look for directories that do not have "*no follow links*". If they do have no follow links then this listing is only for branding.

3.  List where the website's keyword phrases are relevant to topics within the directory.

4.  Only submit to free directories. Most paid directories have proven to be of little value and should be ignored.

Information can be submitted manually or there is submission software on the market that will automatically make the submissions to directories.

The benefit of automatic submission software is that the information is entered only once, the software does the rest. One drawback to most automatic submission software is that it does not always narrow down the categories of directories like a human can do by submitting manually.

> **HINT:** Always manually submit to directories because then the exact category can be chosen.

Every directory has guidelines for submitting information. Most directories require a URL, email *address*, and a brief description of what the organization does. Most allow the selection of a category into which the information should be entered.

## Steps to Manually Submitting to a Directory

Manual submission to directories is very simple. Just follow these steps to ensure that the listing is as good as it can be.

1. Have the information available electronically so that it can be copied into the directory. The following information is usually required: the company's URL, a contact name, email, and phone number along with a brief blurb on what the company offers, what makes this company different, the company's locations, and any other pertinent information that would be helpful to a visitor wanting to learn about this company.

2. Create a password and username so that when returning to update the information, the directory will know that the updated information is trustworthy.

It can take months before the submitted information is listed in a directory and before any traffic to the website increases as a result of that submission. Be patience.  Every directory takes a different amount of time to list the information.

---

**HINT:** Always enter an *email* so that the directory can contact a real person with any questions about the information.

---

One directory which should always get a submission is **DMOZ,** the Open Directory Project (*www*). It is considered the premier directory in the online marketing world and as such Google and others pay special attention to it.

To list information in DMOZ, follow these simple steps. (DMOZ contains categories for almost any business)

### Steps to Submitting to DMOZ

1. Enter *www* in the URL address space.

2. Choose a *category that DMOZ offers.* Be sure to select the category that best matches the organization's product/service offerings.

3. Follow the online instructions and finish the submission of the website.

> **HINT:** Don't submit information to a directory multiple times on the same topic. It won't speed up the process and could seriously hurt the chances of getting listed.

## Submitting Articles to Directories

Submitting articles to *article* directories is a good way to build links as well as a personal reputation. Almost all article directories allow links to be placed in the article. Visitors will follow the link and if they like the article, they may contact the author directly. The best thing that can happen to an article is that other websites use the article and *repurpose* it for other sources.

> **HINT:** Request that the article include a name, email, and website or blog URL even if it has been repurposed. Be sure to get credit for the article.

The key to getting attention for articles is to write about something current and something that people want more information about. Never make personal references in the article, most services have a section where authors can talk about themselves and promote anything.

In order to get started, here are a few places where articles can be submitted at no cost. (See Figure 6-1)

Figure 6-1 Where to Submit Articles

| URL | Name | Speciality |
|-----|------|------------|
| www.articlebase.com | Articlebase | everything |
| www.articlegeek.com | Article Geek | everything |
| www.ezinearticles.com | Ezine articles | everything |
| www.goarticles.com | Go articles | everything |
| www.212articles.com | 212 articles | everything |

Submitting articles is a great way to gather vital links and brand identity for products and individuals.

Let's take a look at other ways to accomplish the linking effect - the **online press release**.

## Online Press Releases – the News

Press releases in the online world (called online press releases) are an effective way to maximize exposure with less effort and to get more "**eyeballs**" looking at a company's information.

Prior to the Internet, press releases were written on paper and sent via the United States mail directly to editors and reporters who were on the lookout for new products and interesting news to put in their publications. They were static press releases and contained text which that had a limited audience. Such press releases generally appeared only in publications and magazines.

The goal of writing an online press release is to describe problems with which the audience can identify and to offer an immediate solution. The release should be entertaining, informative, and have a "*water cooler*" effect that excites readers to discuss the story as more than just news.

These online press releases are shared with more than just editors of magazines; they are useful for obtaining links and awareness of particular products and services.

## Best Practices for Online Press Releases

1. Keep the information concise

Online press releases (OPR) cater to Internet audiences who are interested in factual information, not opinions. **OPR**s should be between 400 to 500 words. OPRs greater than 500 words may lose a reader's attention and may not produce results.

The average reader reads at a speed of 200 words per minute. If the OPR is 600 words long, then it typically would take the reader three minutes to read. Since most readers lose attention after two minutes, the last 200 words may never be read. Limit Keep the number of words to 400, so that the time to read it does not exceed the reader's attention span.

2. Avoid All Caps and Exclamation Points

When potential customers see an *online press release* with all capital letters in either the headline or summary it is LIKE SEEING A CRAZED SALESPERSON YELLING AT YOU TO PLACE YOUR ORDER, NOW! Using capital letters in the online world is considered to be the equivalent of shouting. This is not only annoying to the reader, but tough on the eyes. All caps are not appropriate either.

Use initial caps only for each word in the headline and summary. Use lowercase characters in the body of the OPR and the About Section.

Exclamation marks ("!") convey that the OPR is advertising. **Distribution services** will not run any OPR that appears to be advertising.

Remember the headline is a statement of fact and not an advertisement. A preferred headline in an OPR for diet pills might be "*Amazing Diet Pills Allow Women to Lose Twenty Pounds in a Week.*"

3. Keep the OPRs informative and newsy

Focus OPRs on topics that have value, news, or can help the consumer's life to be better or easier. Avoid creating releases that update older announcements. Avoid mentioning pricing and distribution locations. The reason why these topics should be avoided is it makes an OPR more of an advertisement than an information article.

4. Avoid Abbreviations

Using abbreviations can confuse potential customers. They may not know what the abbreviations mean. Therefore, it is better to avoid them entirely. Most customers do not know what DFR (Delaware Federal Reserve), AMR (Annual Mortgage Rates), and FPL (Fixed Price Loans) mean.

5. Utilize links

These are not links on a golf course, but links that create paths to the web site for potential customers and reporters. These links also provide a method for other websites to connect to the website.

> **HINT:** Never direct all links to the home page. Search engines view this technique to be SPAM. Instead, direct links to different web pages in order to optimize traffic and increase sales.

6. Write in the Active Voice

Write an OPR in the active voice and in the most conversational manner possible. It should seem like a friendly chat. An OPR that is too technical or written like a research paper may drive potential customers away.

7. State the Benefits to the Visitor

Give the visitor a reason to purchase a product or service. Highlight the strengths of the product or service and the weaknesses of the competition. This comparison is a major selling factor. OPRs which clearly state benefits are valuable sales tools and not just self promotion.

8. Tell People about your Company

Include information about the company so that prospective customers can become familiar with both the company and the management. Remember the old saying, "*People buy from people (companies) they know.*" This is true for any product or service. Visitors that purchase goods or services on the Internet like to know about the vendor because this provides reality within a virtual world. Always include a section called About the Company.

9. Use Keyword Phrases for Visitors to Find You

One of the goals when writing an OPR is to include keyword phrases which make it easy for searchers to enter them into a search engine query when researching a topic. Include keyword phrases which describe what the company does and are common search terms for that product, service or industry.

10. Include a Call to Action

Including a **call to action** in the body of the OPR is the best way to lure prospects to a website.

11. Target potential customers

Direct press releases so that they can be targeted toward visitors who might need your product or service. Do not limit the distribution to journalists and reporters. OPRs help direct potential customers to the website and ultimately generate sales.

---

**HINT:** OPRs are usually written with a text editor or word processor. Submission to a distribution services is accomplished by cutting and pasting parts into a distribution template.

# Entering Information into Blogs – Word of Mouse

Another way to direct traffic is to write blogs. Blogs are basically an easy to enter information that accepts any message (*post*) that relates to the focus of the blog. Some blogs are business related, some personal, and some are entertainment focused to name a few.

Blogs do not judge whatever is written. There is no right or wrong entry only the opinion of the person writing the blog (*the blogger*). Blogs look for opinions only.

The main purpose of a blog is to send visitors to a website. The more posts one makes to a blog (the more information one enters) the better the chances that visitors to the blog will go to that poster's website. So, the first motive for using blogs is to send traffic to a website.

Blogs are an easy way to get exposure and send traffic to a website. The nature of a blog is that it is created by an individual's posting on a topic. The better the posting, the more popular the blog is and the more traffic will be sent to that website.

Finding the right blog is easy. Just follow these simple steps.

## Steps for Choosing the Right Blog

1. Only focus on blogs that are relevant to the specific product or service being promoted.

2. Look for blogs that have posts updated on a weekly basis or less. If a blog hasn't been updated for a month or two, chances are that blog doesn't have much traffic, and as such, it won't bring much traffic to the website. Valuable blogs are those blogs that are often updated.

3. Pick blogs that show the comments of its bloggers. By viewing the comments of the bloggers, a lot can be learned about how the blog handles the topic, what is acceptable, and the style of the blog. When in doubt, read the entries for a while before posting.

4. Only pick blogs that have "*do follow*" links otherwise these posts produce no links.

It is simple to find blogs that will work for you. Let's find a blog about "*basketballs shoes.*"

Simply enter this information into the Google search engine

*"basketball shoes + blog"*

Look at the blogs that turn up in the first two pages on the
search engine results page (SERP). See Figure 6-2.

---

Figure 6-2 Searching for Blogs in Google

---

Pick *blogs* that have the most frequently posted material and
the largest audience.

Blogs are looking for material that will make them more
popular and attract visitors. Therefore, blog owners are very
careful about what is posted. Only post information that is
appropriate. Posts that are over the top or are not in tune to
what the blog accepts will be deleted or not posted at all.

### Best Practices for Blogging

1. Only post information that is appropriate for the particular blog.

2. Always use correct spelling and grammar when blogging.

3. Always include information that will allow a visitor of the post to click through to the website, thus, building traffic. Valuable information includes: an email address, website, and any information that makes it easy to find the company or more information on the product or service being offered.

Let's look at another method of driving traffic to a website – *forums*.

## Forums - Places to Contribute

Forums, like blogs, can be effective ways to drive traffic to a website.

Let's first start by looking at forums and selecting the forum that best fits a particular website's needs. Choosing a forum is simple. Just follow these guidelines.

### Guidelines for Choosing Forums

1. Pick a forum that caters to a specific topic. Forums are selected in Google by typing "*baseball+forums*" in the query

box. All forums that match this topic appear in the Google's search engine results page.

2.  Choose forums, like blogs, that are active. Selecting a forum that has few members does not help drive much traffic. A forum that has hundreds of members can drive an enormous amount of traffic to the website.

---

**HINT:** Look at the number of *threads* for a particular topic. This number indicates how many members participate.

---

3.  Look at the links on a forum. The best forums to choose are those that do not have "*no follow*" links because they will not allow the links to go to any website.

A sample list of forums for the topic "*baseball*" appears in figure 6-3.

---

Figure 6-3 A sample listing for baseball forums

---

Once a forum is selected, *register* by creating a *user name*, *password*, and email account.

Most forums have a **signature file**. That file contains information that is displayed after every post is entered. Having a website URL and a link to the website information is deemed valuable.

### Best practices for posting in Forums

1. Present posts in an informative way. Never hide advertising material as information. Forums are created to exchange informative information on specific topics and not for advertising purposes.

2. Follow the etiquette of the forum. When uncertain of the exact etiquette, spend some time reading other threads to see the form and style.

3. Always be truthful and offer useful information.

4. Never enter posts that are fluff like "*That's good*" without referencing the topic or the person you agree with.

5. Offer opinions on the subject or cite a reference in the news or on the internet.

> **HINT:** The reason information is entered on a forum is to build credibility and a reputation for a particular field of knowledge.

## Getting results with social bookmarking

Search engines produce traffic to websites, but there are additional ways to build links and drive traffic to a website – one method is **social bookmarking**. Social bookmarking is similar to making a website appear in a **favorite** list. Having a website appear in a favorite list is a nice way of always getting to a website without requiring the URL to be memorized. It's fast and quick. Now imagine being able to share important or interesting **bookmarks** with everyone on the Internet. That's what social bookmarking is all about.

## StumbleUpon.com

One website that utilizes social bookmarking is **StumbleUpon.com**. StumbleUpon.com is all about having members recommend websites they like. These websites are then voted on by other members who give the website thumbs up or thumbs down. StumbleUpon.com members can also email the website to friends for their votes.

Membership is free and StumbleUpon.com has a simple **toolbar** that can be **downloaded** and installed to make the recommending process easy.

Figure 6-4 displays the StumbleUpon.com toolbar.

Figure 6-4 StumbleUpon.com Toolbar

Once a website is submitted to the StumbleUpon community, the user can vote "*I like it*" or "*I don't*" by clicking on the thumbs up or down icon. If a website is popular, a **pop-up** window appears that enables a link to be added and the website is entered into the StumbleUpon.com database for other visitors to visit.

> **HINT:** A technique to use is _**bookmarking**_ one's own website to get it into the StumbleUpon.com directory.

There are many _**social sites**_ on the Internet that accept articles, bookmark websites, or focus on special topics that may be appropriate for a particular company. To find a listing of social sites just enter in Google, "_social sites_" and hit enter. A listing will appear; then the ones that most closely match a company's offering can be pursued.

## Promoting a website offline

In addition to the online techniques that can be used, there are a number of _**offline promotions**_ that can help promote website traffic.

Think about all the prospective customers in the world. Wouldn't it be great to capture all that traffic? This can be accomplished by including a company's email address and its website URL in all the company's printed literature and in anything that advertises the company.

The website should also be on included on business cards, letterhead, postcards, and newsletters.

In this way, the website will always be visible to all potential customers who wish to obtain additional information.

## CHAPTER 7:

# Measuring Website Activity

**Chapter Contents**

- Google Analytics™ Dashboard
- Visitors report
- Measuring keyword phrases
- Measuring landing pages
- Measuring overall website performance

Up to now the focus has been to generate traffic and improve the performance of a website. Now, the focus shifts toward how to measure the results from these efforts and correct anything that falls below expectations.

The easiest way to measure a **website's performance** is to place an **analytics software** package on that website. **Google Analytics** is my choice because it is free and easy to use. All that is required is to **register** for the software and then placing the **analytics code** on every web page of the website that you need to measure. The rest is up to Google Analytics.

Google Analytics has the flexibility to perform multiple measurements that can help to analyze and correct a website's performance.

It can measure the number of visitors to a website during a given period, the average length of time each of them stayed, which pages are the most appealing, and more.

## Google Analytics Dashboard

Let's look at a Google Analytics™ *dashboard* to view the most common information that is displayed. See Figure 7-1.

Figure 7-1 Google Analytics dashboard

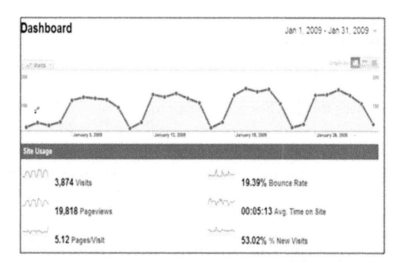

Information on a Google Analytics™ Dashboard:

- Time period – the time period for the reports displayed in the top right hand corner.
- Visitors for the month –the daily visitors for this time period
- Visits –the number of visits for this time period
- Pageviews – the average total number of pages viewed for this time period.
- *Pages/visit* – the average number of pages viewed per visitor (pageviews/number of visitors) for this time period
- Bounce rate – the average visitor **bounce rate** for the website during this time period
- Average time on site – the average visitor time on the website during this time period
- % new visits – the % of the total visitors that represent the % of new visitors during this time period

---

**HINT:** It is important to understand that the absolute figures reported for each period are not the most important numbers; the trend, the changes between each time period is what matters most.

---

**HINT:** A common time period to choose for your analysis is monthly. Start with the 1st of the month and stop at the end of the month.

---

To illustrate this point, consider a traffic measurement made in February of 12,000 visitors compared to March's number of 12,500 visitors. The important trend is that there is a 500 visitor increase during this time period. Google Analytics analyze what contributed to this increase and how to capitalize on it.

The opposite situation occurs when the February traffic remains at 12,000 visitors and March's traffic is 11,300 visitors. Google Analytics analyzes what contributed to this decrease in traffic and pinpoint the problem to fix it.

Let's start by looking at the most common reports that are generated from Google Analytics to measure **website performance**. They are as follows:

## The Most Common Reports from Google

1. Visitors
2. Traffic Sources
3. Keywords Phrases
4. Landing Pages
5. Exit Pages

Let's understand each of these reports.

1. Visitors – this report reports on the number of visitors arriving at a website during a specified time period. There is no distinction of their origin or whether they were new or returning visitors.

## Why the Visitor report is important

If the number of visitors between two given time periods
declines, this downward visitor trend may indicate that
something is wrong within a website or the external forces that
draw visitors to it. Google Analytics provides information to
understand the problem and locate the source of the decline.
The same holds true for increasing visitors.

Figure 7-2 contains a sample visitors (traffic) graph for March.

Figure 7-2    Visitors Report for March

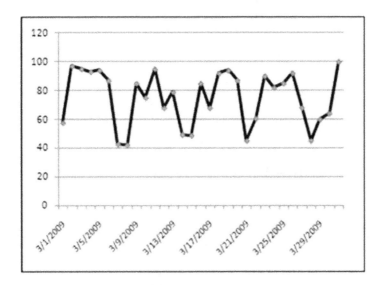

2. Traffic Source – this report indicates where the visitors to your website originated from. It shows whether the visitors arrived at the website through search engines, by entering the URL directly into their browsers, or from other sources.

## Where visitors originate

Knowing where visitors originate is an important *metric* to understand. It tells which sources are producing traffic and which are not. The results could be important in making the decision about where are the best places to promote a product or service.  It would make sense to promote a product offering on the sources that generate the most traffic and to pull back from those that are not as productive.

Table 7-1 shows the number of visitors to a *website* from their source.

Table 7-1   Sources of Website Traffic

| Top Traffic Sources | Visits | Page/Visit | Avg. Time on Website | % New Visits | Bounce Rate |
|---|---|---|---|---|---|
| Direct - typing in URL | 3,500 | 3.92 | 1.44 | 51.54% | 43.00% |
| Google | 1,632 | 4.13 | 1.46 | 61.76% | 37.50% |
| Yahoo | 142 | 4.98 | 1.50 | 58.45% | 28.80% |
| MSN | 43 | 5.07 | 1.34 | 65.12% | 30.23% |
| AOL | 39 | 8.69 | 3.54 | 53.85% | 10.26% |

3. Keyword Phrases – this reports on the number of visitors that came to the website through various keyword phrases that were entered through search engines and other sources.

## Which Keyword Phrases draws visitors

This report indicates which keyword phrases draw visitors to a website. This report helps pinpoint which keyword phrases don't generate traffic.  They can be eliminated or better optimized to increase traffic.

Table 7-2 displays (fictitious data) the keyword phrases that draw visitors to Evan's website.

Table 7-2 Top Keyword Phrases that Produce Website Traffic

| Top Keyword Sources | Visits | Page/Visit | Avg. Time on Website | % New Visits | Bounce Rate |
|---|---|---|---|---|---|
| basketball shoes | 2,600 | 4.72 | 3.55 | 70.00% | 13.00% |
| baseball shoes | 1,950 | 4.10 | 2.50 | 65.00% | 25.00% |
| discount basketball shoes | 845 | 2.11 | 1.50 | 54.00% | 18.00% |
| team gear | 777 | 1.30 | 1.30 | 59.00% | 27.00% |
| buy basketball shoes | 633 | 2.00 | 1.10 | 33.00% | 44.00% |

**Note:** The top drawing keyword phrase to Evan's website is baseball shoes, followed by basketball shoes. (This data refers to a fictitious website - Evans Shoes)

4. Landing Pages – this reports on the breakdown of visitors for each page web page. This report helps determine which web pages are the most popular and which might be problem web pages.

## Where visitors go

It shows which web pages were visited and the number of visitors. This measurement indicates the visitor behavior on that visit. **Behavioral data** includes; the length of the visit, which web pages were of value, and how the length of time on a web page compares to the average time a visitor spent on other web pages.

Table 7-2 shows which landing pages were visited, how many visitors left instantly (bounced), and the various **bounce rate** for that landing web page.

Table 7-2   Landing Page Visited Report

| Top Landing Pages | Entrances | Bounces | Bounce Rate |
|---|---|---|---|
| basketball shoes | 3,580 | 1,459 | 40.75% |
| baseball shoes | 865 | 425 | 25.00% |
| discount basketball shoes | 663 | 320 | 18.00% |
| team gear | 500 | 100 | 28.00% |
| buy basketball shoes | 350 | 280 | 75.60% |

> **HINT:** Bounce rate is the percentage of visitors to a website or web page who leave instantly.

5. Exit Pages – a report that measures the number of visitors who left from a particular web page along with other data

## Why visitors leave

If a visitor leaves after a few minutes of arrival, this could indicate that the visitor is focused on the product and service. On the other hand, if a visitor continues on to a checkout page, it is even better because that indicates that an order has been placed. If a visitor lands on a particular page and then exits from that page in a few seconds, it could indicate that the visitor did not find what they were looking for or perhaps typed in a keyword phrase that has multiple meanings, and did not see the desired item on that web page.

Table 7-3 shows an **exit page** for Evan's website along with other *metrics* that are important.

Table 7-3    Top exit page report

| Top Exit Pages | Number Exited | Bounces | Bounce Rate | Time on Page |
|---|---|---|---|---|
| basketball shoes | 4,200 | 1,459 | 40.75% | 1.2 |
| baseball shoes | 2,250 | 1,200 | 55.00% | 0.5 |
| discount basketball shoes | 268 | 40 | 14.93% | 4.02 |
| team gear | 129 | 79 | 61.24% | 5.11 |
| buy basketball shoes | 50 | 25 | 50.00% | 1.6 |

The next chapter discusses another type of search – Pay-per-Click. These techniques are different in that they require placing bids on keyword phrases in order to obtain placement. This process is akin to the stock market and is discussed in detail next.

CHAPTER 8:

# Pay-per-Click Campaigns

*Chapter Contents*
- Keyword phrase generation
- Ad copy
- Making ad copy valuable

A Pay-per-Click campaign is another part of Organic Search Engine campaigns. It differs from Organic Search Engine campaigns in that in PPC or Pay-per-Click, the advertiser bids for keyword placement by creating a three line ad copy to induce traffic to a website.

Let's look at some typically tasks of PPC. They are:
- Choosing Keyword phrases
- Writing Ad Copy
- Tracking the results
- Managing a campaign for maximum traffic

Let's assume Google AdWords™ campaign is running and that an account has been setup. The first step in any PPC campaign is to generate keyword phrases for bidding. It is simple to do but certain factors must be considered.

## Keyword Phrase Generation

1. Keyword phrases, discussed in Chapter 2, are the terms that best represent a website and its product offerings.  In a Pay-per-Click campaign (paid campaign or *paid placement*) beside a budget for bidding, the keyword phrases that bring in the greatest amount of traffic are also needed.

> **Note:** Unlike Organic SEO, an advertiser pays for the privilege of being on the top positions on the 1$^{st}$ page of Google. The difference here is that with PPC the results can be achieved sooner compared to several months to a year with Organic SEO.

### Best Practices for Creating Keyword Phrases

1.  Use plurals of words because they are more competitive. More searches are performed each month for the plural of a keyword phrase. When it comes to bidding being more competitive also means being more costly. If traffic is needed, spend the money for the plurals. It is worth it.

2.  Choose keyword phrases that consist of two, three, or more keyword phrases.  Although these specific keyword phrases tend to generate less traffic, they generate more *conversions (call to action)*.

3. Optimize the landing page (where these keyword phrases are directed) to make it appear exactly as the keyword phrases describe. A visitor, looking for information about *medical schools* will not be happy to land on a page that only discusses graduate schools. This result requires the visitor to put additional effort for medical schools. Be specific to generate the best conversions and the lowest bounces.

Once keyword phrases are created, the next step is the ad copy.

## Ad copy

An **ad copy** in Google AdWords is limited to three lines. The first line can be up to twenty five (25) characters long and the maximum for the other two is thirty five (35) characters each.

### Best Practices for Creating Ad Copy

1. Make the ad copy relative to the search term.
   Google gives ads that are relative to search terms higher quality rates than those that are not.
2. Use keyword phrases in the first line and as many times as possible in the remaining other two lines.
3. Always put the brand name or sales pitch in the lines following the first line.
4. Always capitalize the first letter of each word in the ad copy.
5. List the benefits of the product/service offering before the features. Benefits sell, features are just easy.

> **HINT**: A lawnmower that can cut your entire lawn in 27 minutes is more appealing than a lawnmower that never needs a bag to change. Combining both together, "*Our lawnmowers can cut your entire lawn in just 27 minutes without changing bags*", is the best choice.

Figure 8-1 shows a **Google AdWords** campaign ad for "*basketball shoes*"

Figure 8-1  Ad Copy for Basketball Shoes

**Basketball Shoes Sale**
Buy Your Basketball Shoes on Sale
Evanshoes.com carries all Brands
Evanshoes.com

Getting started with a **campaign** is a simple process; begin with the right strategy to achieve maximum clicks without paying maximum dollars.

There are two factors that affect an ad's position. They are:

- How much the bids are for a given position

- The ad's **quality score**

The price paid for a keyword phrase determines what position the ad will appear.

If the going rate for the keyword phrase "*basketball shoes*" is $4.25 per click for position #2 on page one, the only way it can be lower is by having a higher quality score.

The quality score is based loosely on the following:

1. How well a landing page is optimized for the keyword phrase.

Keyword phrases that are optimized for specific terms don't disappoint visitors. On the other hand, if they don't find what they were searching for on that landing page and leave without taking any actions, this would indicate that the landing pages have not been optimized. Google keeps track of this and factors it into the quality score as a negative value if they all bounce.

## Making ad copy valuable

In a Google AdWords campaign ad copy that contains at least one of the keyword phrases that matches a query entry has a higher value. Ads that have no keyword phrases have lower ad quality scores and are usually charged more to bid for the same position.

2. The number of high quality links to a landing page helps the Google AdWords quality score. A higher quality score is given because more links to a landing page establishes **authority** for that landing page. The higher the authority, the more Google values this web page and the higher value it assigns to the ad copy that points to that landing page.

3. The performance of ads at certain positions effects how Google values the quality score.

4. When an ad is at a certain position (basically 1-10 on page one) its **Click-thru-Rate** (**CTR**) is a certain percentage. Google keeps track of similar ads that were at that position, basically their CTRs. If an ad copy has a higher CTR than another ad copy at that page, Google raises the higher CTR's ad quality. If the ad copy is lower than what others have achieved for CTRs then Google lowers the ad quality rating.

Pay-per-Click values a Meta Description tag on the landing page. If the Meta Description tag on the landing page describes the landing page in an accurate way with keyword phrases, then the ad copy quality is raised. Obviously if not, Google lowers the quality score.

Always optimize a Meta description tag for the highest quality.

Keeping all this in mind, let's pick a bidding strategy.

### Best Practices for Bidding in a PPC Campaign

1. Research your competition. Spend some time to see what positions that they have paid for and what keyword phrases they use. Try to only research the competitors who are in the top five positions on page one.

---

**Hint:** The campaigns of the leaders in the Pay-per-Click campaigns will show what ad copy works and what keyword phrases they use. This tool is called Spyfu at www.*spyfu*.com.

---

Always pay for the number one position on page one. Being on page one, position one shows the world that an ad has value and visitors perceive the ad copy as a "*premier provider*" as opposed to someone that is simply running ads.

2.  Always run a daily time for displaying the ads. Setting the ad to run between 7:30 AM to 5:30 PM is enough of a window that visitors who are serious about the product will click on the ad copy. Sometimes leaving an ad running 24 x7 pulls up SPAM. (unless the ad is also focused on the international market)

3.  Always set a daily and monthly budget. In that manner the PPC spending can be bounded.

All that remains is to manage the ongoing Pay-per-Click efforts.

### Rules to weed out the non performers

1.  Pause keyword phrases that don't get clicked on after a two month period.

2.  Increase the bid or position for keywords that are non performers to determine if a turnaround can happen for these non performing keyword phrases.

3.  Eliminate or rework ad copy that is seldom viewed or has a low quality score.

> **Note:** Ad copy that has a low viewed rate hurts a campaign and should be eliminated or reworked to get higher quality score ratings.

4. Remove any keyword phrases after a two month period that have a low CTR from the campaign.

Keyword phrases that are associated with low click through rates actually hurt a PPC campaign. Google views the CTRs and averages all of them together to arrive at an average rate. If there are two or three keyword phrases that have a high quality CTR then a lower keyword phrase CTR can bring down the overall quality that Google assigns to your campaign.

Running a Google AdWords campaign is a lot of work but it can produce results more quickly and more controllably than any other type of online marketing. Be sure to consider a Google's AdWords campaign anytime a new product is launched or as an adjunct to an Organic Search Optimization campaign.

## CHAPTER 9:

# Delivering Content with Podcasts

*Chapter Contents*
- Introduction to Podcasts
- What is a Podcast?
- Generating Traffic
- Topics for Podcasts
- Creating Podcasts
- Podcast Process

## Introduction to Podcasts

Marketing via a *podcast* is a new concept that has taken off in the last two years. *Podcasting* is a way of getting a message across by bringing focus to a particular product/service and building traffic at the same time.

Many podcasts are free for the consumer. Podcast costs are minimal (in basic form, they require only free software and a good quality microphone) and because of their nature, distributing recorded conferences, political commentary, or publishing business articles is a more cost effective means of sending material.

Podcasts maximize exposure of information on a social site or on a private website. The more people that listen to a podcast about a business, the better the chances are that traffic will be driven to the website associated with that podcast and that the podcast will help to establish a brand identity for that organization. The most important factor of podcasts is that they are subscription based. That means that people have to request podcasts and download them.

## What is a Podcast?

Podcasts are low-cost *syndicated* digital audio files that are created in an **MP3** format. A podcast is an audio mini-program broadcast over the Internet. Podcasts can be downloaded and listened to on any MP3-compatible digital music player. One of the earliest devices for podcasts was an Apple iPod. Thus, it got its name - podcast.

Think of podcasts as blogging with audio (MP3 files) instead of text.

Individuals can subscribe to lists of podcasts and choose to download them and then listen to them while commuting, exercising in gyms, or anytime they have access to a device that can play an MP3 file. This is in contrast to traditional Internet radio where music or other audio content is streamed at particular times and is not always available without Internet connections.

## Generating Traffic

The reason one should create a podcast is simple - traffic. It's like the proverbial word of mouth, spreading "*the message*" about anything and everything in the online marketing world like wildfire.

Once an audience finds value in the podcast they always want more. This information can be done once or a weekly or monthly occurrence. Now they are hooked. Podcasts allow their producers to know who is out there and what their interests are because they subscribe. Targeting an audience with specific podcasts allows one to get new prospects, to keep existing customers interested in the product, to expand a well known brand's reach, and to strengthen customer relations.

Podcasts eliminate SPAM because their audiences must download podcasts through subscription services or request them through particular websites. Therefore, this audience is a self-selected, interested group, which distinguishes podcast from other kinds of campaigns like unsolicited emails.

Podcasts are a one-to-one communication vehicle that any business can use to connect with small niche audiences to communicate new ideas, products and concepts. In essence - a website traffic producer.

## Topics for Podcasts

Podcasts can handle any topic that an audience searches. Here are nine sample *podcasts* that create opportunities to increase product awareness.

### Sample Topics for Podcast

1. Reviewing Products – a podcast can review anything and everything on the market that is relevant to a target audience. Getting product recommendations from this audience drives traffic to the website.

2. Demonstrating Expertise – a podcast can highlight an organization's expertise in a particular area.

3. Case studies with podcasts – a podcast can talk about a case study of how other organizations solved their problems by using a particular product/service offering.

4. Industry trends – a podcast can discuss and forecast trends. Searchers want to know what is ahead so that they can

capitalize on the future.  In addition, searchers are interested in knowing how a product/service can help ease their concerns about the future.

5. How to guides – a podcast can act as a how-to guide. Anything that helps to make a person a better salesperson helps a person to fix a roof, to save money with repairs, etc. is sure to bring traffic to a website for further information.

## Creating Podcasts

As mentioned before, podcasts are simple and inexpensive to create. Let's see exactly what is required to create a podcast. What is needed is podcast software, a Personal Computer, access to the Internet, and a microphone. That's all. And the really good news is that all of that can be purchased for between $30 and $120 dollars.  The software is free.

Distributing podcasts (getting people to hear them- called **syndication**) is done through the Web. That requires an **RSS feed** (Real Simple Syndication) or downloading them directly through sources like:

 *iTunes*, by Apple Computer, PodOMatic (URL- www.podomatic.com/),  all podcasts (URL – www.allpodcasts.com), and other podcast sources.

## The Podcast Process

1. Download the software by using a browser and entering http://audacity.sourceforge.net/

See Figure 9-1. It displays the website of audacity to download the software.

Figure 9-1 Audacity Software

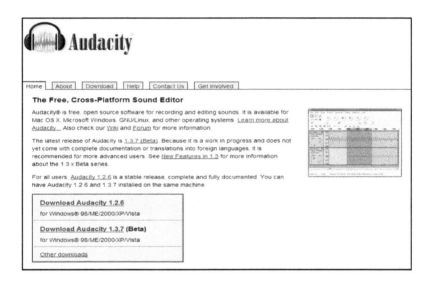

1. After the software is downloaded and configured, write a script for what the podcast is going to be.

> **Hint:** Limit a podcast to ten minutes or less for best results.

2. Once the podcast is finished and the quality is satisfactory, submit it to one of the above sources for syndication.

The more proficient one becomes at creating podcasts the easier it will be to drive traffic to a website. Some companies produce a series of podcasts and that way can always be assured of an audience for their new product or service offerings.

CHAPTER 10:

# Improving Traffic with Social Sites

### Chapter Contents

Social media networking is another method in addition to search engines to bring traffic to a website. In the beginning, *social media* was basically for personal use, but now they have evolved into a series of tools that businesses can use for traffic and *branding*. Through social media networking users can explore interesting products and services that they become exposed to on their social networks or hear about from friends. These groups collectively can view a company's products and/or services and spread the word to their friends, distribute the website URL or links, and, depending on the conventions of any particular social site, vote on what they like the most. There are several social media websites that are effective in getting products and services a place in their networks. The first of these popular social media networks is *Facebook.com*.

## Facebook can create an identity

The purpose of Facebook.com  is to allow individuals or businesses a **profile** on a network that other users can view, comment on, and distribute to their own network.

To create a Facebook page, simply type the URL, www.facebook.com, and select the option at the bottom of the page as shown in Figure 10-1.

Figure 10-1 Creating a Page on Facebook.com

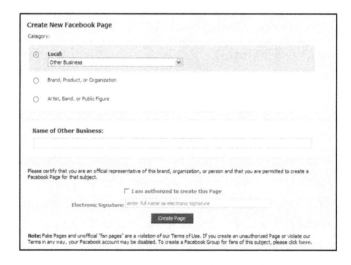

Select a category from the drop down box and give the business a name. The name of Evans Shoes was chosen and the product description of sports/Athletics was chosen. Check the authorization button and the **page** is done.

At this point, the following information can be entered.

The date a business started, write-up about the business, a URL, and a mission statement. This information almost fills up the page. Next, if there is a *logo* for the business, it can be added to the page.

Now enter photos in the photo album. In the case of Evans shoes, a photo of basketball shoes, baseball shoes, team gear, etc, can be entered. Along with the photos, a short description or caption can be entered for each photo.

The application section of Facebook is a great feature. Applications are anything that people will get involved in like an application to see if a person is a good candidate for a credit card. After working with the application, the thought is that the person will network with other users or fans and share that application. The overall effect is to bring people to a particular Facebook page and then ultimately to a corresponding website.

Finally, Facebook has the ability to run advertisements that are custom tailored to the demographics of a particular target audience.

Businesses can run contents and opinion polls on the business page. Once a business has built up a fan base with sufficient volume, the fans can voice their opinions on specific features of new products or opinions about topics in general. Some topics could include. "*Is the caffeine in coffee good for your health?*" The results from an *opinion poll* like this one could lead enormous traffic to a particular website especially if it is a coffee business or a medical facility that conducts such surveys.

The key in producing a Facebook page is to acquire a large number of fans (people loyal to a particular site) who can help spread the word around their own networks.

Another social networking website is *Twitter*.

# Using Twitter

Twitter is a social networking site where visitors send text posts, called **tweets**, (usually up to 140 characters) from any device like mobile phones or computers that can be read by others and where they can get updates about friends like where they are or what they are doing.

### How Does a Business Use Twitter?

Twitter works well with some businesses. For example,

- Retail clothing business that is running an end of season special for closing out past season's products, can tweet (messages) to the community about the sale.

- Real estate businesses can send out tweets about new homes coming on the market.

- Automotive dealers can send out tweets about the new models of cars that are coming on the market, and invite the readers to come in and test-drive the car.

There are countless ways that Twitter can be used for business.

# The major function of Twitter

The major question on everyone's mind about Twitter is, "*What are you doing?*"

This can get people talking. As a business, it is essential to go further and offer valuable advice. Companies like grocery chains share links that they think would be valuable to their target community and travel companies always share travel tips. The key to success on Twitter is informing the community but not selling them.

Here are some ways that Twitter can be used for business.

**Ways Twitter can be used for business**

1.  Comment on new product tweets that may be in a similar product or service space.

> **HINT:** Add points of value rather than just saying company's XYZ product has more features and is more impressive.

2.  For retail businesses, Twitter can be used to broadcast weekly specials in a similar way that a grocery store tweets their daily specials to their customers.

*YouTube* is another social media networking website that produces website traffic. Let's look at YouTube and how it produces traffic.

# YouTube

If promoting a business through a video is appealing then YouTube is a great way to go. YouTube requires that all users *register*, but the good news is that registration is free.

YouTube allows almost any video, in various formats to be **uploaded**; the only restriction is that files must be under 100 MB and less than ten minutes long. This is an easy barrier to overcome. Simply register the first file as part one and the next file as part two and so on. To create a YouTube video, it can be up to 300 MB of video and 30 minutes in length.

YouTube has all types of video on their website, from businesses selling soap, trailers for new movies, CEOs talking about buying their products, and more. There are millions of viewers and if a video becomes popular, it can push traffic to any website. YouTube videos provide maximum exposure.

> **HINT:** Tag the video with keyword phrases. Remember Evans Shoes and their product basketball shoes. Putting basketball shoes and Evans Shoes' URL in a video about playing basketball like the pros, can generate a tremendous amount of traffic.

## Best practices for using YouTube

1.  Whenever a video is put on YouTube always enter keywords in the description field and link it back to the website. Use some of the keyword phrases generated in Chapter Two to put them in the **tags** of the video and the description fields.

2.  Mention a company name, product and service description early in the video and at the end. If a viewer doesn't watch the entire video they can still see this information.

3.  Focus on the main theme of the video. Common themes can be buying the right automobile insurance, laundry detergent, or how to do something using product xyz. Have the company's name mentioned at the beginning, but don't sell until the end. Selling should consist of just mentioning where the company is located (*www.company name*) or placing a footer on the bottom of the video which states "*this video is brought to you by*" on the last screen of the video.

4.  Don't use profanity in the video. There are videos that feature it, but the audience should be treated with respect and the video should be kept professional. Extreme humor or adult situations may offend some viewers and tarnishes a business image.

5. Make a video good quality. A video that blasts music to the point of being annoying or that is filmed in a dark setting may get bypassed by the target audience and give the wrong impression of a company.

# Using Digg.com for visitors

*Digg.com* has thousands of visitors daily to their website. Digg.com is essentially a social website that features news and events, articles, and just about everything else on their website. These topics are broad based; a glance the Digg website appears to have info on everything.

Top producing stories on Digg.com are those that feature:

- Technology
- World and business reports
- Breakthroughs or problems in science
- Gambling
- Lifestyle issues
- Sports
- Offbeat or bizarre stories

## Steps to Work with Digg

1. Start by signing up for a free Digg account by going to www.digg.com. Register and select a category of interest.

2. Be familiar with the top stories on the website by reading them. Note stories with the highest number of Diggs ratings. These are significant stories to emulate.

3. Write a sample article for Digg and have friends Digg it. That way you get the feel for writing.

4.   Make as many Digg *friends* as possible. Ask them to vote. It's Important to increase Digg votes.

5.   Become a frequent Digg commentator and vote on as many Digg sites as possible.

> **Hint:** Becoming an active member of the community is the key to collecting friends. Those friends will vote for your story and spread the word around the Internet.

6.   Build a community Digg environment.

7.   Include an email address and your website  on everything that you write about.

Getting a story on the front page of Digg takes some effort, but it is well worth it. Some front page stories have drawn over 10,000 visitors over a period of a few days.

## Using del.icio.us to get tagged

The Del.icio.us website (www.delicious.com) is another social networking website that works with tags or bookmarks. It organizes information by bookmarked tags and shares those tags with any searcher.  Del.icio.us helps by first tagging information and having other users pass it along to other interested parties or by appearing in the Del.icio.us.com database to be viewed on the home page.

The bookmarking works as follows:

1.   Del.icio.us uses tags or bookmarks that are single words that describe the content of the article – for example, "*tattoo*" in the case of an article titled "*how to find tattoo designs.*" These single words (tags) can describe one of the many of thousands of topics that are stored in their database.

2.  Every time an article or story is bookmarked that information is stored in the Del.icio.us's database. The tags can be passed around among friends. Rather than bookmarking the information on an individual computer. The importance difference is that this information is bookmarked on a website on the Internet that allows it to be shared. The goal is to have information shared with the largest audience. These bookmarks are passed around until the traffic has grown.

3.  Go to *www.delicious.com* and register. Register by entering a username, password, and email address, you're finished the **registration** process. Once registered is completed, any user can also visit the del.icio.us homepage and search for specific bookmarks (tags) that interest them or create new ones.

When users request information about tag topics, they pull up all the articles from the database that relate to these bookmarks.

## Final words about social sites

In addition to the social networking websites mentioned, there are hundreds of other social websites that focus on a myriad of topics ranging from art to how to select a new camera for taking pictures.

Because of the sheer volume of people visiting  these social websites daily, the odds are that at least a handful of visitor's interested in content about a specific topic will visit the website or pass the information some way. Featured articles on the homepages of any of these directories could generate hundreds of new visitors.

CHAPTER **11**:

# Avoiding the Search Police

### Chapter Contents
- Techniques to avoid
- Hidden text or links
- Keyword stuffing in Meta Titles or Meta Description tags
- Over submission
- Duplicate Header tags
- Doorway pages
- Link farms

In this book, there have been several techniques described to optimize a website and produce traffic; from **On-Site Optimization** to **Off-Site Optimization**. These efforts require work and time to implement but in time those efforts will be rewarded with higher ranking and more traffic. There are a number of new "**Black Hat**" or SPAM techniques regularly invented to trick search engines into bringing more traffic to a website. Search engines are continuously on the lookout for these practices and will penalize websites by taking away the offender's website **page rank** or banning those websites that are caught employing techniques that they deem to be unacceptable or illegal.

To avoid this type of SEO punishment, it's important to avoid the tactics described in this section.

## Techniques to Avoid

1. Hidden Text or Links

The excessive or repeated use of content, keyword phrases or links invisibility on a web page to achieve higher SEO ranking is deemed illegal by search engines and can result in a website being delisted from the major search engines. The "*stuffing of information*" is accomplished by placing this information in the same color as the web page background (hidden to blend in) so that it blends in and is invisible to humans and only detectable by search engines.

2.  Keyword Stuffing in Meta Title or Meta Description Tags

The repeated use of keyword phrases in a Meta Title or Meta Description Tag to achieve higher SEO ranking is deemed illegal by search engines and can result in a website being delisted from the major search engines. The "*stuffing of keyword phrases*" is accomplished by placing keyword phrases repeatedly in the Meta Title Tag and Meta Description Tags (HTML).  See figure 11-1.

---

Figure 11-1 Stuffing of Keyword Phrases in a Meta Title Tag

---

```
<title>Basketball Shoes Basketball Shoes Basketball Shoes
Basketball Shoes</title>
```

3.  Over Submission

Submitting a website to search engines or directories too often is referred to as **over submission** and most search engines consider these to be SPAM techniques.

> **HINT:** Submitting a website more than a few times per year puts a website at risk of being considered SPAM. The only time a website should be resubmitted to directories is when it has been categorized in the wrong category.

4.  Duplicate Header tags

Header tags on a web page highlight content headings. As previously discussed, the H1 header tag is considered the most important and should not be implemented more than once on a web page. The reason that multiple H1 tags would be repeatedly implemented is to enhance a particular keyword phrase or phrases for better ranking. As with the other techniques, this is not well accepted by the major search engines and results in a penalty.

5.  Doorway pages

These are pages created specifically for search engines and are hidden from website visitors. These pages are full of keyword phrases, links, and more. Using **doorway pages** can result in a website being **banned** so avoid using these techniques.

6.  *Link Farms*

This involves the setup of numerous websites for the express purpose of linking to other websites (often unrelated websites) to boost a website's rankings. The idea of **link farms** now includes social networking websites and blogs. Link farm links associated to a website is bad, but linking a website to a known link farm is considered a very serious offense and usually punishable by banning the website.

In general, always be on the lookout for any schemes that solicit or promise links to a website that seem too good to be true. Their claims never offer a guarantee that the results they promise will ever happen. It is better to focus only on techniques that are known to increase a website's value and efforts that search engines award with full credit for the hard work.

## CHAPTER 12:

# Gary's Odds N' Ends

## Chapter Contents
• Websites with Page Rank of 10
• Other uses for Google.com

In this chapter I've included a list of odds and ends that consist of websites with a ranking of 10 and other uses for Google that perform specific functions, but that are little known. Some of the Google uses are tools may help answer questions about *"What else does Google know about my website?"* or *"Does Google have information about similar websites?"* These odds and ends may prove useful just for the public record.

## Websites with a Page Rank of 10

Google rates each website with a page rank. Page Ranks run from 1 to 10. Page Rank is a measure of authority and trustworthiness. Google itself has a page rank of 10, but so do other websites. Here are those websites. See Table 12-1.

Table 12-1 Websites that have a Google Page Rank of 10

| Name | URL |
|---|---|
| World Wide Consortium | http://www.w3.org/ |
| CNN Network | www.cnn.com |
| USA government | www.usa.gov/index.shtml |
| Adobe Flash Player website | http://get.adobe.com/flashplayer/ |
| The government of India | http:india.gov.in/ |
| Adobe reader website | http://get.adobe.com/reader/ |

## Unusual Uses for Google.com

Did you know that Google.com is a very flexible search engine. Believe it or not, it can be used to learn the time difference between two points, synonyms for a search terms, and the time around the world. (Google™)

1. Time difference between two points

For example, to see the time difference between Boston and Chicago, enter,

> *What is the time difference between Boston and Chicago?*

2. Movie reviews

For example, to find movie reviews for *Cat on a Hot Tin Roof,* enter,

> *Movie Review of Cat on a Hot Tin roof?*

3. Geographical locations for any area code

For example, to find the geographical location for area code 617, enter,

> *What are geographic locations for area code 617?*

4. Weather in any part of the country

For example, to find out the weather in Chicago, enter,

> *What is the weather in Chicago?*

5. Finding related websites

For example, to find other websites that are similar to your website, enter,

*related: www.websitename.com*

6. How does Google view a website?

To find out how Google views your website, enter,

*cache:www.websitename.com*

7. Google has information about websites

For example, to see what information Google has on a particular website, enter,

*Info:www.websitename.com*

There are many other interesting things you can do with Google.com just experiment around and you will be surprised at the results.

# GLOSSARY

## Number

**2G** – (**S**econd **G**eneration wireless telephone technology) is the technology used by many wireless devices like the Apple iPhone 2G.

**301 REDIRECT** - a command that instructs the hosting server to move a website or web page permanently to a new location. This is the preferred method of redirecting for most web pages or websites. It usually takes anywhere from a few days to a month for the 301 redirect to take effect and have your website or web page moved.

**302 TEMPORARY REDIRECT** - a command that indicates to the hosting server that the website or web page has been found, but it is temporarily located at another URL. As it relates to SEO, it is typically best to avoid using 302 redirects because some search engines struggle with redirect handling.

**3G** – (**T**hird **G**eneration wireless telephone technology) - a faster technology recently used by mobile devices like the Apple iPhone 3G.

**404 CUSTOM ERROR PAGE** – a page created so that when visitors enter a misspelling or a web page that has moved they are directed here to stay on the website and instructed to try again rather than receiving an error and leaving a website.

**404 ERROR NOT FOUND** – the code that the server sends to the search engine that indicates that the website or web page specified was "not found."

**% NEW VISITORS** – this is the percentage of new visitors to a website over a particular period of time determined by their IP address or other measures.

**% RETURNING VISITORS** – this is the percentage of returning visitors to a website over a particular period of time determined by their IP address or other measures.

# A

**ABOVE THE FOLD** – a term traditionally used to describe the top half of a newspaper page.  In terms of search engine marketing, this describes where a segment of the results appear on the search engine results page (SERP). It signifies the area of a computer's screen content that is viewable without scrolling downward.

**A/B TESTING** -  the process of randomly showing to a visitor two versions of websites landing pages, called A and B. Normally reserved for Pay-per-Click campaigns but recently it has shown value in Organic search campaigns as well. The A version is your current landing page and is the control page. Version B is the landing page with some elements that are different.  When these are measured, notice is taken which one produces more results (conversions) and they are then incorporated into the original landing page.

**ACTIVE X** – Microsoft's technologies and services that allow web browsers to download and execute Windows programs to run in Internet Explorer.

**AD BLOCKING** – equivalent to blocking commercials on TV. Here Web advertisements are blocked from appearing on your web page.

**AD COPY** - refers to the three lines of text in a Pay-per-Click campaign (text ad) used to obtain better placement for a keyword phrase.

**AD QUALITY SCORE** – refers to the rating that Google has given to an ad copy in Google AdWords campaign based upon the number of keywords used in the ad, the rating of the landing page, and other factors. Google rates the ads from 0 – 10 (10 is the highest).

**ADOBE ACROBAT** – a no cost, downloadable software program from Adobe Systems that allows PDF files to be viewed. PDF files have become the method of publishing on the web.

**ADOBE SYSTEMS** – commonly referred to as Adobe, located in San Jose, California, is a company that produces computer software. Adobe was founded in 1982 by John Warnock and Charles Gesckhe after they had left Xerox. The company's focus is on multimedia, creativity, and Internet software products. In December of 2005 Adobe acquired Macromedia, a software company with similar products. Adobe is best known for Photoshop, Dream Weaver, Acrobat, and PDF creation (**P**ortable **D**ocument **F**ormat file) software products.

**ADSENSE** – Google's contextual advertising (paid search) network.

**ADWORDS** – Google's advertisement and link auction network. This is a pay-per-click (bid for a term) keyword campaign. Keywords and phrases are targeted and sold on a cost per click basis in an auction.

**AFFILIATE** – a revenue sharing opportunity between online merchants/advertisers. The arrangement usually consists of one company being associated with an organization that has entered a marketing and/or sales arrangement to sell another company's offerings.

**AGGREGATOR** – a website that gathers information related to particular topics on the web. This information originates from many sources such as websites, RSS feeds, or other sources on the Internet.

**AIM** – (**A**merica **O**nline **I**nstant **M**essaging) allows anyone to chat online with another person. AIM can be done via a computer or a wireless device.

**AJAX** – (**A**synchronous **J**avaScript) an HTML technique that allows a web page to request data from a server without requesting a new page to load.

**ALERTS** – a service available from various online news sources and aggregators that will automatically send updates on various user selected topics whenever those topics appear online, in specific blogs, or in the specified news source.

**ALEXA TRAFFIC RANK** – an online service (Alexa.com) that measures traffic for millions of sites on the Internet in a way similar to the one Nielsen uses to rate television shows. The Alexa number indicates how many websites are rated above the site being measured.  Thus, a lower Alexa number indicates that a web site has few competitors which outrank it. This ranking system is owned by Amazon.

**ALGORITHM** – a proprietary mathematical equation that a search engine uses to determine the relevance of a web page to a searched word or phrase. This formula is constantly upgraded and kept secret to the public so that no one can get an advantage by knowing it.

**ALT TAGS** – a way for search engines to read, by inserting HTML code, the text contained within certain files such as PDF (**P**ortable **D**ocument **F**ormat file), flash images, and other types of files.

**ALTAVISTA** - the first searchable, full text database on the Internet. It was created by Digital Equipment Corporation's Western Research Laboratory for the purpose of locating files on the public network and launched on December 15, 1995 as altavista.com. The name Alta Vista was chosen because the company was located in Palo Alto. In October of 1999 Alta Vista dramatically changed their marketing approach and upgraded their algorithm. Ultimately, this resulted in loss of market share and mind share. Later, AltaVista was purchased by Overture. Overture was then purchased by Yahoo.

**AMAZON.COM** – the largest Internet retailing website. Amazon.com is known for the products it carries which include books, DVDs, music CDs and games. Amazon also owns a number of websites including Alexa.

**ANALYTICS CODE** – a small amount of JavaScript tracking code that is installed on the web page or pages that need to be measured. Typically measurements include how visitors arrived on a page, the length of time they stay, where they go after leaving, etc.

**ANALYTICS SOFTWARE** – a tracking system that works by installing a JavaScript tracking code on each web page that includes data. The system then tracks the behavior of visitors to the website. Most analytics measure factors such as visitor page views, visitors to the website, sources of traffic, bounce rate, visitors arriving at specific landing pages, new and returning visitors, keywords, and conversion statistics from visitor to buyers for a website.

**ANCHOR TEXT (TAG)** - an HTML tag that is used to label text in a link to another document or webpage or to bookmark a particular web page.

**AOL** – (**A**merica **O**nline) a popular web portal which merged with Time Warner.

**API** – (**A**pplication **P**rogramming **I**nterface) represents a computer system or application which allows requests to be made of it by other programs and allows for data to be exchanged. This is commonly referred to as a "black box" where certain actions at the input produce a predefined action at the output.

**APPLE, Inc.** - Apple Inc., formerly called **Apple Computer Inc.,** a California corporation established on April 1, 1976. Apple Computer, Inc. dropped the Computer from its name when it branched out past computers into consumer electronics, iPod, and software products. Apple (as it is called) is best known for its Macintosh computer, the iPod, the iPhone, and various software titles.

**APPLE IPOD** – one of the most popular brands of portable media players designed and marketed by Apple Inc. It was first launched on October 23, 2001.

**APPLICATION** – a computer program (software) that provides the means (a tool) to accomplish a task.

**ARCHIVES** - backups of posts or entries in an index page that are organized by either category or date.

**ARTICLE** - a story, essay, report, or opinion that appears in newspapers, journals, the Internet, or similar places.

**ASK** - a search engine, originally named Ask Jeeves (exemplified by a butler logo), owned by Interactive Corp and powered by Teoma. In early 2006, the term Jeeves was dropped from the name.

**ASP** – (**A**pplication **S**ervice **P**rovider) any company that provides computer-based applications and/or services over the network. Those services may include providing software, hosting (place where the application is residing) or support. Some companies that offer this service do so free of charge and make their money through advertising.

**ASP HOSTING** – (**A**ctive **S**erver **P**age Hosting) a server type scripting environment from Microsoft.

**ATTACHEMENT** – a file or group of files that is included in an email message. Every email program has an attachment feature where files can be sent.

**AUDIO BLOG** – is another name for a podcast.

**AUTHORITY** – the amount of trust that a particular website has relative to a search query. Authority comes from the relevance and ranking of incoming links and other websites that link together.  For example, the query "milk" can be associated with a "dairy cow" website because a dairy cow website has a lot of authority. While the website for "*garden tools*" has no authority for query "*milk.*"

**AVATAR** – is an icon or graphic that represents a person in a cartoon-like manner in a way that person chooses to be represented in places like chat rooms or virtual worlds. Avatars need not be accurate representations of the people they represent and some avatars are dogs, aliens, talking heads, etc.

**AVERAGE TIME ON SITE** – this is the average of all the time all visitors spend on a website determined over a particular time period.

# B

**B2B** – (**B**usiness to **B**usiness) is a term for companies whose target market for the selling of goods or services to other businesses.

**B2C** – (**B**usiness **to** **C**onsumer) is a term for companies whose target market for the selling of goods or services to the end consumer.

**BACK LINKS** - links (hypertext code) that point to a particular webpage on a website from an outside source. These are also referred to as inbound links.

**BANDWIDTH** – the volume of data, expressed in kilobits per second (_kps_), that can be transmitted in a given time period over a communications channel. The measurement is similar to how much water can travel through a hose in a given span of time.

**BANNED (BANNING)** – the action which search engines take to remove a website from their search engine index because of actions that violate the guidelines for ethical practices. When a website is banned, the action can usually be reversed by removing the techniques that were used originally to trick the search engines. These unacceptable practices are called Black Hat techniques and can consist of SPAM, hidden text, doorway pages, etc. If after repeated warnings the website still does not follow the search engines' guidelines, the ban may become permanent.

**BANNER AD** - usually a graphic, typically 468 pixels wide and 60 pixels tall (i.e. 468 x 60), advertisement placed on the top of a website page. When users click on the ad links, they are linked back to the advertiser's specified web page.

**BASELINE ANALYSIS REPORT** – see Benchmark Report.

**BEBO** – a social network founded by Michael and Xochi Birch in January 2005 and subsequently purchased by AOL in March 2008 for $850 million dollars.  The name Bebo is an acronym for "**B**log **e**arly, **b**log **o**ften". Its purpose is to allow its members to stay in touch with their college friends, connect with friends, share photos, discover new interests and just get together regardless of where they are located. It is used in many overseas countries including:  Canada, the United Kingdom, and Ireland.

**BEHAVIORAL DATA** – is the data on how predefined groups of people, with common behavioral patterns, react to specific target ads or messages.

**BEHAVIORAL TARGETING** – the process of targeting groups of people who have commonalities with particular target ads or messages. These people may be similar because of the way they react to certain messages in the online world or may be in the target group for gender, age, or websites they frequently visit. Behavioral targeting takes into account shopping patterns and other characteristic which these people have demonstrated online.

**BENCHMARK REPORT** – a report (also called a SEO baseline report) used to document a website's standings (rank) for a number of factors including page rank, keywords, page views, traffic, etc.

**BEST PRACTICE** – a technique or methodology of accomplishing a function or process that has been proven to be superior to all other known methods to produce a desired result through experience and research. SEO is often performed in a best practice way in order to accomplish superior results.

**BID** – the process of competitively submitting and resubmitting the highest price a purchaser is willing to pay to increase or maintain an ad's position in pay per click (PPC) results. The advertiser pays an amount for each visitor that clicks on the advertiser's ad. Bids are conducted in an auction environment where higher bids effect placement of the ads on the search engine's result page. The higher the bid the closer to top of the search engine results page the ad appears. If visitors do not click on an ad then the advertiser is charged nothing. Hence, the name was called pay-per-click.

**BIDDING** - the process of competitively submitting and resubmitting the highest price a purchaser is willing to pay to increase or maintain an ad's position in pay per click (PPC) results.

**BINGO CARD** – a prepaid postcard that was inserted in a magazine by the publisher to enable readers to check off the product that they wanted more information about. These products can be any advertised products or services listed in the magazine.

**BLACK HAT** – techniques when used in conjunction with Search Engine Optimization are considered by search engines as unethical and should be avoided as part of any search engine optimization campaign. Black Hat, as the story goes, claims its name from the practice of outlaw cowboys in the Old West wearing black hats while the good guys wore white hats.  The techniques employed in Black Hat include cloaking, doorway pages, keyword stuffing, non relevant links, and hidden text behind web pages.

**BLOG** – a contraction of the words we**b log** and is a website that is regularly maintained by an individual, called a blogger. Blogs are gaining popularity because they can be updated easily by people using available software that requires little or no technical background.   The entries in a blog, called Blog entries, usually consist of text, although some contain music, video, audio (podcasts), are displayed on the blog in reverse-chronological order.  The content on blogs can include anything from descriptions of events, personal information such as news articles, diaries, comedy, views on the economy, new product ideas, or any other type of material. Two popular ways to create a blog are to use Blogger.com from Google or Wordpress.com.

**BLOG AGGREGATOR** – a website that gathers information related to particular blogs on the web. This information originates from many sources such as websites, RSS feeds, or other sources on the Internet.

**BLOG CONTENT** - the content on blogs can include anything from description of events, personal information such as news articles, a diary, comedy, commentary, views on the economy, new product ideas, or other type of material.

**BLOG ENTRIES** – are the entries in a blog. They can consists of text, although some contain music, video, audio (podcasts), are displayed on the blog in reverse-chronological order.

**BLOGGER** – is an individual who makes entries into a blog.

**BLOGGER.COM** - a popular website (www.blogger.com) owned by Google that allows individuals to create their own blogs free of charge.

**BLOGGING** - a new entry made to a blog.

**BLOGOSPHERE** – is the universe of blogging (making entries to a blog) and bloggers (the individual who makes them).

**BLOGROLL** – a list of sites displayed in the sidebar of a blog. The sidebar displays a list of the other blogs that the blogger reads regularly and, therefore, act as a kind of recommendation of those blogs.

**BOOKMARK** – the act of saving a website address or content in a browser or a social book marketing website. Microsoft Internet Explorer bookmarks are referred to as favorites. The main purpose of a bookmark is to have frequently viewed websites or web pages in an easy to find place for later reference.

**BOOLEAN SEARCH** - most search engines include AND with a query, requiring results to be relevant for all the words in the search query. A Boolean search allows AND, OR, or NOT to be specified as well.

**BOUNCE RATE (BOUNCES)** - a measurement of the quality of traffic arriving at a website. The bounce rate measures the percentage of people who come to a website and leave "instantly." Visitors are said to bounce if their stays on a website are only long enough to view a single page and leave or if they stay on a website for a very short period of time usually four seconds or less. A high bounce rate indicates that the site failed to fulfill the visitor's expectations.

**BRAND** - the recognized image, symbol, graphics, or reputation a company's name or logo has to a great many people.

**BRANDING** – the process of building a recognized image for a company that is known to many people because of the name. Branding is developed through controlling customer expectations and the social interactions between customers.

**BRAND IDENTITY** - is the summation of name and visual appearance of the brand. It is the process by which consumers recognize a product or service and differentiate it from its competitors.

**BREAD CRUMBS** – a website's navigation tool that is usually displayed in a horizontal line above the web page's content. Bread crumbs allow the users to see where the current page is relative to the Home page or other web pages. For example, if

a user is on a portfolio page, they may see
"Home>Products>Portfolio."

**BROADBAND ACCESS** – is fast access to the Internet.

**BROAD MATCH** – when a paid search campaign bid specifies
that a search result will lead to a match only when an entire
keyword phrase matches in its entirety and that this is the only
situation that will register as a click.  For example, if "*fur scarf*"
is typed into a paid search query for a broad match bid, then
the only time a match occurs is if the entire phrase was bid.
Entering "*scarf*" would not trigger the broad match for the key
phrase "*fur scarf.*"

**BROKEN LINK** - refers to any viable link (path) that was
programmed to lead to a document, image or webpage when
selected and does not. Most broken links (links that go
nowhere) usually result in displaying "page not found," a time
out or any other type of error.

**BROWSER** – an Internet tool used to view websites, web
pages, access news feeds, content, and documents on the
Internet by downloading them to your computer. (Also known
as a web browser)

**BULLETIN BOARDS** - the equivalent of public notice
bulletin boards that allowed for Internet online collaboration.
Users were able to connect with a host computer in order to
enter text (post) and read messages.

**BURN** – slang for making (burning) a CD-ROM copy of any
type of data, whether it is music, software, or other data.

**BUZZ** – a lot of talk about topic with frequent mentions of the subject online, in a community, or on a social network.

**BUZZFLASH WEBSITE** - a popular social media website that solicits political news stories from the public. These stories are then ranked by the members of the site and displayed in rank (position) order by Buzzflash.com.

**BUZZWORD** – the overuse or obscurity use of technical or sector specific words or phrases. Popular buzzwords in the past were "*user-friendly*" or "*virtualization.*"

# C

**CACHING** - the process of copying web pages by a search engine into its index. When a user searches the web, that person is really searching the particular search engine's index for a listing of all the web pages stored (**cached**). This index is a file that the search engine uses to sort web pages by relevance (importance) and other factors.

**CALL TO ACTION** – an advertisement that encourages a visitor to take immediate action to fill out a form, sign up for a newsletter, or purchase a product or service or some other way to interact with a company.

**CAMPAIGN** - a campaign refers to specific activities that create interest in purchasing a product or service. Pay per click (PPC), banner ads, search engine optimization campaigns, and more are all campaigns that achieve this objective.

**CATEGORIES** - pre-established ways to group content.

**CCGM** – (**C**ompensated **C**onsumer **G**enerated **M**edia) the practice of paying users to perform a task such as making a post on a blog site or writing some content on a social media site, etc.

**CGI** – (**Common Gateway Interface**) allows HTML pages to interact with programming applications. Programming applications can consist of forms, counters, and guest books, and more.

**CHAT** – the interaction between people, in real time, on a web site to exchange text in a conversational manner.

**CHAT ROOM** – a website for live, online conversation in which any number of people can type a message to each other and communicate. Chat Rooms are usually focused on particular topics but some are designed to provide a venue where people can meet. The messages in the chat room appear on the screen next to the person's log-in information.

**CHICKLET** – the nickname applied to the small orange button for the RSS feed button (small square with waves) that is used subscribe to a newsletter, news, etc.

**CLICK** – a depression of a computer mouse button that moves to a given location as defined by the link or action taken.

**CLICK FRAUD** - the deceitful practice of bidding in a pay per click (PPC) campaign for the purpose of increasing the costs for legitimate advertisers thus generating revenue for those affiliates serving the ads.

**CLICK-THROUGH** – the process of clicking (selecting) a link usually on an online advertisement or other paid campaign and following that through to a website or landing page.

**CLICK THROUGH RATE (CTR)** – is a calculation performed in Google AdWords campaign or other paid search campaigns. The calculation consists of the number of time a user clicks on an ad divided by the number of times an ad is displayed. It is a measure of the effectiveness of an advertisement.

**CLIPART** – refers to ready to use graphic files that can be used in websites, brochures, blogs, etc.

**CLOAKING** – the action of tricking a search engine into indexing a different version of the web page than what appears on the website. The version that the search engine sees with cloaking has keywords stuffed in it and contains other features that will boost its website ranking. All search engines consider cloaking unethical (black hat) and as such will penalize the website caught performing cloaking.

**CLOUD COMPUTING** - is done over a combination of networks, servers, and connections called "the cloud." The purpose of cloud computing is to allow users to access software and services directly over their computers without installing packaged or shrink wrapped CD's.

**CMS** (**C**ontent **M**anagement **S**ystem) – is a system designed to simplify the publication of content, the words and phrases that appear on Web sites. The main benefit of such a system is to allow content to be placed on a website without a technical knowledge of HTML or other techniques to upload files.

**COLLABORATION** – the sharing of information with people across the Internet by using blogs, forums, chats, email, podcasts, and social media.

**COMMON GATEWAY INTERFACE** – a way to move traffic by using software between a web server and other machines or software running on that server.

**COMPETITIVE ANALYSIS** – is an analysis of the competition's website. The analysis looks at factors from the competition that may benefit the website that offers a competing product or service. Factors that may prove helpful include keywords, links, and traffic sources.

**CONNECTIONS** – the way users gain access to the Internet. Usually the speed of the connection is what matters. Dialup, Broadband, and Cable are a few of the ways that people connect to websites on the Internet.

**CONTENT** – the words and phrases that appear on a website.

**CONTENT NETWORK** - all networks of Internet locations that serve (display) paid advertisement based on a visitor clicking on a keyword related to the page a visitor is viewing.

**CONVERSIONS** – web traffic that fulfills a pre-established goal, such as purchasing of a specific product or filling out a registration form, etc.

**CONVERSION ANALYTICS** – a measurement of all Organic (free clicks) and paid search engine traffic. Analysis can include keywords used in each search, specific landing page paths and the resulting conversions.

**CONVERSION PATH** - the way users progress, through website visits, banner ads, product review, testimonials, that result in the purchase of products and services.

**COOKIE** - information which a website places on a visitor's computer so the visitor's preferences will be remembered on subsequent visits.

**COST PER CLICK (CPC)** - the cost paid to the provider of a paid search campaign by an advertiser when a user clicks on a particular term or sponsored link that takes the user to a web page of the advertiser. Pay-per-Click keywords may cost an advertiser anywhere from $0.10 to over $35 and up depending on the popularity of the keyword triggering the ads.

**COST PER LEAD (CPL) -** the total cost paid to obtain a lead from a paid campaign. For example, if an advertiser received four clicks on a particular campaign and the total cost is $100 for these four clicks, when one of these clicks turns into a lead then the cost per lead can be calculated to be $100. A lead can be construed to be a completed contact form, a survey or email address or any other call to action.

**COUNTER -** a web service used to count the number of visitors to your website.

**CRAIGSLIST.COM** – founded by Craig Newmark, Craig's list is a central network of online communities featuring largely free classified advertisements for a variety of services and products such as jobs, products, cars, housing, personals, and more.

**CRAWL (CRAWLER)** – an action by a search engine that is carried out with accordance to a script. The act of crawling is carried out according to the links that are in a website sitemap. The purpose is to obtain all the latest content on web pages on a website.

**CRAZYEGG.COM** – a software service that simulates where a visitor goes to during a website visit by a graphic representation.

**CRM** – (**C**ustomer **R**elationship **M**anagement) is used for tracking traditional sales processes including lead generation, sales forecasting, measuring pipeline value, and more.

**CROWD SOURCING** - an expression associated with broadcasting a work request to a community of skilled and unskilled workers on a global basis. The first people who respond usually get the work.

**CSS** – (**C**ascading **S**tyle **S**heets) a language that informs a website how a given web page will be displayed through the use of specifying control fonts styles, color, graphical layout, etc.

**CYBERSPACE** – the total connections with human beings through communications and computers without geographic boundaries.

**CYBERSQUATTING** – the practice of purchasing popular trade-marked domain names or common misspellings of popular brand names (like apple.org, goggle.com, or cokekola.com) to either sell the domain names or pull traffic through a misspelling of popular brand names to redirect that traffic to another website.

# D

**DASHBOARD** - the area on your blog software that allows posting, checking traffic, uploading files, managing comments, etc.

**DATA TRANSFER** - the total amount of outbound traffic leaving a website. Typically measured in gigabytes per second (Gbs).

**DATABASE (s)** – a structured collection of information (data) that is categorized by records containing fields that are stored and searchable by keyword phrases in specific fields.

**DEAD LINK** - is a connection to another location (link) which takes the user nowhere. Search engines view this as a quality problem.

**DEL.ICIO.US** - a social bookmarking website owned by Yahoo, that allows users to create and store searchable bookmarks of web pages and later share these bookmarks with other users or to organize (tag) and manage them.

**DELISTED** – the act of banning a website from listing on a search engine's database because of some illegal or violation of a search engine's rules.

**DEMOGRAPHICS** - the physical characteristics of a population such as age, sex, marital status, family size, education, geographic location, and occupation.

**DESCRIPTION META TAG** - an HTML code, usually a few sentences in length and no more than 150 characters long including spaces, that informs search engines about the focus of an individual web page. It is helpful in Search Engine Optimization because it serves to classify each web page's topic thereby simplifying the task of categorizing that web page in the search engine's index.

**DIGG (DIGG.COM)** - a social website focused on content where people submit stories, how-to articles, news, etc. to be shared with other users. All content submitted is voted on by the Digg community and the highest voted content is placed on the first page.

**DIRECT** - when a user arrives at a website by typing a URL into the browser rather than entering the site from a link, advertisement, or whitepaper.

**DIRECTORY-** a research tool that compiles a list of websites along with brief descriptions and contact information. It differs from search engine directories because the listings are submitted by humans and then they are reviewed by human editors as to their acceptability according to the directory's guidelines. Entries that do not meet the criteria are rejected. Those that are accepted are then placed into specific categories on the directory similar to a phone book listing.

**DISTRIBUTION SERVICE** – is a service (free or paid) for submitting online press releases to social news websites or other websites in order to provide product or service announcements.

**DMOZ** – (The Open Directory Project) owned by AOL and the largest and most comprehensive human edited directory on the web. It is constructed and maintained by a vast, global community of volunteer editors.

**DNS PROPAGATION** – (**D**omain **N**ame **S**erver Propagation) refers to the amount of time required after a new domain is registered to be recognized on the Internet. The length of this process is about 24 hours, during which time the domain will not be viewed by others.

**DOGPILE** – a special search engine, developed in 1996 by Aaron Flin that only searches through other search engines like Google, Yahoo, Ask, and others. When it encounters multiple search results it filters these results to only display a single listing. Dogpile.com was sold to Go2net and later to Infoscape.

**DOMAIN NAME** – is the name that identifies a website's location (address). This is the name a human enters that has to be transferred to a computer language, an IP addresses, for the computer to process. For example, the website address, *www* has a domain name of **john.com**.

**DOMAIN NAME SERVER** - a computer (server) that translates human viewable URL's into computer recognized language called IP addresses. This occurs every time a user requests a page from a website.

**DOMAIN SUFFIX** - the domain name suffix that indicates which top level domain (TLD) web site belongs to. There are only a limited number of such domains. For example: gov - Government agencies; edu - Educational institutions; org - Organizations (nonprofit); mil – Military; com - commercial business; net - Network organizations; ca – Canada.

**DOORWAY PAGE** - is an entry into a website other than through a homepage. The major use of this type of page is to spam search engines or represent a website's content as being more than what it is. Search engines prohibit the use of doorway pages and will, in most cases, penalize the website if this practice is discovered by them.

**DOWNLOAD** – to transfer a file from one computer to another computer electronically.

**DREAMWEAVER** – a web development authoring application, by Adobe Systems that offers a **W**hat **Y**ou **S**ee **I**s **W**hat **Y**ou **G**et (WYSWYG) type of output. Users can easily create a website that contains graphics and multimedia elements. Dreamweaver was originally developed by Macromedia and purchased by Adobe Systems in 2005.

**DROP DOWN MENU** – a vertical clickable list that appears on the screen with many choices. When a choice is selected, the menu executes the choice.

# E

**EARTHLINK** - an Internet service provider headquartered in Atlanta, Georgia.

**ECADEMY** – is a business social network that was established in 1998. Ecademy.com's purpose is to let business people connect to one another through online networking at business events. It provides one-on-one meetings in a community setting where business people can advocate for, connect with, and generally help one another.

**ECOMMERCE WEBSITE** – a website used to sell information, products, or services over the Internet.

**EMAIL** – (**E**lectronic **Mail**) messages transmitted over the Internet. An email can be simple text, embedded images in text, or a combination of text and attached materials like documents, images, links, or other content.

**EMAIL ADDRESS** – a unique location identifier (virtual address) where email messages can be sent and received. An email address consists of name, @ symbol, and domain name. For example, *onlinemarketingterms@gmail.com* is an email address.

**EMAIL MARKETING** – the promotion of goods or services through the use of sending of email to a merchant's target audience.

**EXACT MATCH** – is a form of keyword phrase matching in a Google AdWords or other Google campaign where the ad is only displayed when a user enters a search term that "*exactly matches in the correct order*" the phrase specified. For example, in a Pay-per-Click campaign an exact match is specified for "basketball shoes", it would appear in the Pay-per-Click campaign (or other Google campaigns) with the keyword phrase enclosed by brackets such as "[basketball shoes]". A user will only click through to the ad if the keyword phrase they enter is exactly the same, and in the same order without anything in between the keyword phrases, as what was specified. For example, if [basketball shoes] was specified and "*men's basketball shirts and shoes*" is entered, there is no match and the user can not click through to the advertiser's advertisement.

**EXCITE** – an Internet portal that was established by a group of Stanford University students in 1994. Excite.com has had their ups and down from being acquired by @Home networks on January 19, 1999 to being sold to Ask Jeeves on March 2004.

**ENTRY** – a term usually associated with a blog. It is an individual post or article published on a blog.

**ENTRY PAGE** - is a page that visitors arrive at when they enter a website. The entry page may or may not be the home page. An entry page is also called a landing page.

**EXIT PAGE** – the last page that a visitor views before leaving a website.

**EXTRANET** – a private network that uses the Internet protocol and public telecommunications system to securely share business information or operations with internal employees, partners, vendors, or customers.

**EYEBALLS** - the online term for views (or visitors) to video, Pay is the online term for views (or visitors) to video, Pay-per-Click ads, or visitors to a website.

**EZINE** - an electronic online magazine, owned by private people or companies, that can be delivered from another website, RSS feed, or by email.

# F

**FACEBOOK (FACEBOOK.COM)** – a social networking website, founded by Mark Zuckerberg while at Harvard University in 2004, with the purpose of connecting friends and friend's friends. Originally, it was created to connect only college students, but it has expanded to include the general public.

**FACEBOOK PAGE** – is a page on Facebook.com that is used by friends, coworkers, and fans to communicate and post comments.

**FACILITATOR** – a person who helps people in an online group or forum manage their conversations.

**FAQ** - (**F**REQUENTY **A**SKED **Q**UESTIONS) the most often asked questions by the online user about a given company's product or services.

**FARK (FARK.COM)** - a community news and social website founded by Drew Curtis in 1993, that allows users to comment on daily news articles and other items from various websites or submit their own news articles. If their articles are approved by the administrators, these news articles are posted on the main page.

**FARKED** - slang for your server has crashed because it cannot serve up the requested page.

**FARKERS** – members of the online social news website communities called Fark.com.

**FAVICONS** – (**F**avorites **I**con) a small graphic image, 16 x 16 pixels, displayed in the left corner of a website's URL area in a web browser's location and in the favorites menu.  Favicons can increase brand identity when displayed or bookmarked. They can be found in the favicon.ico directory.

**FAVORITES** - Microsoft Internet Explorer's equivalent of a bookmark. Favorites can be saved web pages, websites, or links saved in an organized list that allows for quick access.

**FEED** – a content management system that allows readers to subscribe to content update notifications via RSS or XML feeds for the purpose of reading, viewing, or listening to material from blogs, podcasts, or other RSS enabled websites without visiting each location individually.

**FEED AGGREGATOR** - a client software (resides on the user's own computer) or a Web application which collect syndicated web content such as news headlines, blogs, and podcasts in one single location for easy viewing. (See also Feed Reader, News Reader, and Aggregator).

**FEEDBURNER** - a WEB 2.0 online service, launched in 2004, to allow readers to subscribe to its content. Feedburner.com provides custom tailored RSS feeds and management tools to bloggers, podcasters, and other web-based content publishers for measuring the amount of traffic to a blog and optional advertising. In June 2007, Feedburner.com was acquired by Google Inc. for a rumored $100 million dollars.

**FEED READER** – client software (resides on a user's computer) or a Web application which collects syndicated web content such as news headlines, blogs, and podcasts in one single location for easy viewing. (See also Feed Aggregator, News Reader, and Aggregator).

**FEEDS** – an online web document that is a shortened or an updated version of a web page created for syndication. It is delivered at the user's request, through a Rich Site Summary (RSS) or through Extensible Markup Language XML format through a subscription.

**FIREFOX** – is a no cost, open source Web browser that can run on Windows, Linux and Mac OS X. It is a feature rich browser with capabilities such as an ability to block pop-up windows, tabbed browsing, privacy and security measures, smart searching, and RSS live bookmarks.

**FIREWALL** - a server whose function is to protect a private network website or other websites connected to the Internet from unauthorized access.

**FIRST BLOG** – Justin Hall is credited with creating the first blog while he was attending Swarthmore College in 1994. He called it "*Links.net.*"

**FLAME** – a message or posting directed to a person, company, etc. that is considered hostile or insulting.

**FLASH** – a set of multimedia software tools produced and marketed by Adobe Systems to add animation, interactivity, and video, on web pages.

**FLESCH-KINCAID READABILITY TEST** – a test designed by Dr Flesch and Dr. Kincaid to measure the readability level of words. This is considered the yardstick to indicate the comprehensive difficulty when reading the content on a web page. The higher the F-K scores the lower the reading level.

**FONT** - a character collection (set) from the family of typestyles used in word processing documents or on a website, etc.

**FOOTER** – navigation links and copyright notice that appear on the bottom of a web page or blog.

**FORM** – an interactive section on a website that collects visitor information through its predefined sections. Information such as name, email address, phone number and more is collected and processed by the website. The purpose is to gather information for prospecting, newsletters, and other sales activities. Most website forms are collected through electronic means such as Common Gateway Interfaces (CGI). (See CGI in the glossary).

**FORUM** – an online bulletin board discussion website in which users can have discussions with other people about subjects posted on sections of the forum.

**FRAMES** – an HTML technique for website design that allows two or more pages to be displayed in one browser window. Frames were originally created by Netscape in order to display multiple smaller pages on a single display. Experience has shown that this technique does not benefit search engines because it is harder to navigate correctly through a website and in most cases spiders miss crawling through frames and, as a result, are unable to index the entire website.

**FREEWARE** – software that is available at no charge to use.

**FREQUENCY** - the number of times a piece of information is delivered (appears) to a user in a single session.

**FRIENDS** - contacts on social networking sites whose profiles have been linked to one another. On some sites people are required to accept the link, others are automatically accepted.

**FRONTPAGE** – is a web authoring system by Microsoft Corporation.

**FTP** - (File Transfer Protocol) is the protocol for transferring data between computers.

**FURL** – (**F**ile **U**niform **R**esource **L**ocators) is a free social bookmarking website that allows members to store searchable copies of web pages and share them with others. Each member receives 5 gigabytes of storage space. The site was founded by Mike Giles in 2003 and purchased by LookSmart in 2004.

**FUZZY SEARCH** – a search that finds matches even though words entered into a query are only partially spelled or misspelled.

# G

**GATEWAY PAGE** - pages created to rank high with the search engines but which are not visible to the visitor. Typically these web pages are optimized for particular keyword phrases with the purpose of leading the visitor to another page. This is called a black hat technique.

**GEOGRAPHICAL TARGETING** – the process of targeting where ads, in a pay-per-click campaign, will or will not appear based on the searcher's location. Geo-targeting also has the benefit of costing less than corresponding nationwide campaigns.

**GIF** – (**G**raphic **I**nterchange **F**ormat) an 8 bit-per-pixel or 256 color bitmap image, This format was originally promoted by CompuServe in 1987 to help users minimize the long times associated with the transmitting of graphic files.

**GMAIL** – a free web-based email service, started on April 1, 2004, provided by Google, Inc. In Germany and the United Kingdom it is called Google Mail.

**GODADDY.com** – an Internet domain register and web hosting company that also sells online business related software and services.

**GOOGLE (GOOGLE SEARCH ENGINE)** – is the world's premier search engine that enables users to search websites on the Internet.

**GOOGLE ADWORDS** – Google's major source of revenue from their main Pay-per-Click advertising program.

**GOOGLE ANALYTICS** – a software product offered by Google to measure a websites performance.

**GOOGLE ADWORDS KEYWORD TOOL (GAKT)** – a free utility (by Google) that helps advertisers select which keyword phrases have a sufficient amount of monthly searchers to be used in a campaign to generate traffic.

**GOOGLE FLU TRENDS** - an application that Google launched in November 2008 to provide up-to-date influenza related activity estimates for each of the 50 states in the United States. Google's data closely follows the data from the US Centers for Disease Control.

**GOOGLE PAGE RANK** - a numeric value from 0 to 10 (10 being the highest) that represents how important a website is on the Internet. Google, Inc. calculates that when a page links to another page, it is effectively casting a vote for that other page. The greater number of votes cast for a page, the more important the page must be. Also, the importance of the page that is casting the vote determines how important the vote itself is. Google's Page Rank is a summation of the votes for all of the website's pages.

**GOOGLE SITELINKS** – a method developed by Google about three years ago to augment a website's SEO listing in Organic search results. Google Sitelink allows up to eight additional popular website links to be added to your website's SEO results listings (provided that a Google XML Sitemap exists).

Use Webmaster tools to create a listing of links like the following for the Evan.com website:

Evan.com: Online Shopping for Basketball Shoes, Baseball Shoes, Shirts ..

Online retailer of basketball shoes, baseball shoes, baseballs, logo shirts, logo pants, basketball pumps, and team gear.

www – Cached – Similar pages

| | |
|---|---|
| Basketball Shoes | Basketballs |
| Baseball Shoes | Baseballs |
| Logo shirts | Your Account |
| Inquiries | About Us |

**GOOGLE SITEMAP (XML)** – a way to inform the Google search engine crawlers about the URLs on a website.  A XML Sitemap is to aid Google to do a better job of crawling (not miss any hyperlinks) through a website to index web pages and perform other functions.

**GOOGLE SITEMAP GENERATOR** – a program that generates a Google XML sitemap of all the hyperlinks on a website page.

**GOOGLE TRENDS** – a web tool offered by Google, Inc. that shows the most popular searched keyword terms from 2004 until today. Its URL is Google.com/trends.

**GOOGLE WEBMASTER TOOLS** – a set of tools provided by Google that provides detail reports about a website's visibility and other information on a Google search engine.

**GRAPHIC DESIGNER** – is a person with a graphics arts background who focuses on art, text, digital media, and other visual media for websites, web pages, logos, business cards, etc.

**GRAPHICS** – a picture or image that was computer or human generated (can be scanned from a photograph) and can be placed online.

**GUI** – (**G**raphical **U**ser **I**nterface) a visual representation of the functional code. In this manner an average web user can interface with a database, program, etc.

**GURU** – a person who is viewed as an expert in a specific area. The online world has many gurus or people who profess to be gurus. Caution is suggested to verify that the person chosen is actually a guru.

# H

**HACKER** – a term that has come to mean person who participates in illegal computer or Internet trespassing, but that originally derived from the innovative, exploratory use of technology.

**HEADER TAGS** (**H1** thru **H14**) – a group of HTML tags used to define section headings on a web page. Search engines pay special attention to heading tags because they provide a summary of the topic of that web page and should contain (for SEO purposes) relevant keyword phrases.

**HIDDEN TEXT** – is the process of placing text that is visible only to the search engines in a website's page. This text is embedded in the code or blended into the webpage by appearing in white against a white background. It is used to include extra keywords in the page without becoming evident to the user. Most search engines penalize or ignore URL's from websites that use this practice.

**HIT** – a request or retrieval of any item, GIF images, HTML pages, and JPEG Images, located within a web page. It has no meaning in measuring website traffic. The more relevant metric for website traffic is visits or visitors.

**HITWISE** – an Internet monitor that collects data directly from ISP's (Internet Service Providers) networks. Hitwise.com aggregates information into useable data to monitor and track one's search engine progress.

**HOME DIRECTORY** – the main page of a website commonly referred to as "Home." It usually follows the following name convention, /, www.website name and ext (www.main.com), etc.

**HOME PAGE** – is a website's main page. The Home page contains links to interior pages of the website. The Home page is also referred to as index.html or index.htm. Usually the logo on the top of any interior web page when clicked on will return the user to the Home page.

**HOSTED APPLICATION** – is a software application that is residing on someone else's server.

**HOSTING COMPANY** – is a company that sells physical storage space on its web server to store anyone's website.

**HOTBOT** – one of the first Internet search engines launched in 1996. It still exists today but as a front end to Yahoo.com and MSN.com.

**HTML** – (**H**yper **T**ext **M**arkup **L**anguage) a set of markup symbols or codes inserted in a file for display on a Web browser page. HTML instructs the web browser how to display a website's content and images. Individual HTML code is called an element or tag. In SEO Meta tags, HTML code depicts where to begin the code and when it is to end. HTML is the most common coding syntax used to create web pages and websites. HTML defines how elements of a web page will appear when viewed by a browser.

**HUBPAGES** – a blog website launched in August 2006 that allows its members to create individual content pages on specific topics of general interest. It differs from other blog networking sites because it uses the Google Ad Sense API to administer revenue sharing with writers. Quancast reports that it is the 200th most visited site in the United States and had over 2.9 million worldwide unique visitors in 2008.

**HYPERLINK** - a navigational reference to another document or page on the World Wide Web.

# I

**IDENTITY** – is the personal and financial information about an individual. On the Internet an individual's identity is kept protected from others.

**IMAGE** - a term usually used to refer to an online picture, such as a jpeg or gif file.

**IMPRESSION** - a single view of an online advertisement being displayed. Every time a visitor views a banner ad or a web page that is considered a single impression. The slang of this is "*pairs of eyeballs*".

**INBOUND LINK** - a term used to describe link building methods. A one-way link only comes to a particular website and stops. It consists of a Hyperlink which points to a website without any returning links.

**INDEX** – a collection of websites and web page content that is saved in the search engine's database. This information consists of copies of web pages, titles, descriptions, and keywords.

**INDEXED PAGES** - Search engines scan the Internet for websites and web pages related to keywords entered into their query. When those keywords match the URL's search engines have stored in the indexes of their databases, they list the websites or web pages, in order of importance, in the search results page.

**INFORMATION SEEKER** - any person or persons researching or browsing websites for general information or specific information on an industry, products, and or services.

**INKTOMI** – a California company founded in 1996 by Eric Brewer and Paul Gauthier, UC Berkeley students that provide software for Internet Service Providers. Inktomi.com is currently owned by Yahoo.com.

**INSTANT MESSAGING (IM)** - a way that one can chat with another person over the computer using an Instant Messaging (IM) tool like *AOL Instant* Messenger, *Microsoft Live Messenger* or *Yahoo*. An IM tools allows one user to see whether or not another pre-listed person is available for a chat, and if messages can, therefore, be sent to one another in real time rather than waiting for emails to get information. Problems can arise when people in a group are using different IM tools that don't connect. One way around this is to use a common Voice over IP (VOIP) tool like *Skype* that also provides IM.

**INTERNET** – a worldwide computer network of interconnected smaller computer networks by means of satellite, telephones, and other communication devices using the Internet Protocol (IP).

**INTERNET MARKETING** - allows computers (websites, banner ads, paid campaigns) to interact with a business from any computer or wireless device connected to the place where that advertisement is residing. Internet marketing or online marketing is the only media today that produces prompt results and a good ROI for the money and time spent.

**IP ADDRESS** – (**I**nternet **P**rotocol **A**ddress) a unique combination of numbers assigned to individual computers or networks that communicate over the Internet. The address is a trackable for any computer. The format of an IP address is a 32-bit numeric address, written as four numbers separated by periods. Each number can be zero to 255. For example, 1.168.11.243 could be an IP address.

**ISP** – (**I**nternet **S**ervice **P**rovider) a company that provides individuals and other companies access to the Internet, website building and virtual hosting services. Example: some ISP's are EarthLink, NetZero, and AOL.

**ITUNES** – is a multimedia player software from Apple, Inc. Using iTunes registered users of any iPod-like device can connect to a directory of podcasts, music files, documents, or books.  ITunes acts as an aggregator of podcasts to allow users to subscribe to podcasts.

# J

**JAVASCRIPT** – a scripting language (writing actions) based on prototype-based programming. It is used on a website as client-side JavaScript, and also to enable scripting access to objects in other applications.

**JPG FILE** – (**J**oint **P**icture **G**roup) a popular graphics file format, in which files end with a JPEG, which compresses images to a fraction of their original size. JPG uses an algorithm which is a '*lossy compression*', meaning that the higher the degree of compression, the more resolution is lost from images in a compressed format.

# K

**KEYPHRASE(s)** – two or more word phrase potential buyers would type into a query to locate products and services on a given website.

**KEYWORD COUNT** – a measure of the number of times a keyword or phrase appears in the content of a web page.

**KEYWORD DENSITY** – is an algorithm that is used to determine whether keywords are being overused on a web page. The algorithm takes into account the total number of keywords on a web page divided by the total number of words on a web page. Keyword density is expressed as a percentage value.

**NOTE:** Keyword density should fall between 3% and 9% to be effective in Search Engine Optimization.

**KEYWORD MATCHING** – the process of matching keywords to the query entry in four different ways. Each keyword phrase searched can be expressed as broad matches, phrase matches, exact matches or negative matches in order to redefine the searcher's query into something that conveys the real meaning of the keyword phrase and reduces costs due to irrelevant clicks.

**KEYWORD PHRASE** – is a group of words that search engines use to determine the topic or focus of a website or web page. Their purpose is to categorize a webpage for the purpose of adding that information to the search engine database of categories of all websites and web pages on the Internet.

**Example:** "*Gardening tools*" is a keyword used to categorize a website that sells gardening tools, plants, and supplies.

**KEYWORD META TAGS** – an HTML tag that lists all the main keywords and phrases that are contained on a specific web page. It is still important to a search engine but it is not as valuable today as it was several years ago.

**KEYWORD RANKING INDEX (KRI)** – is a mathematical means to evaluate your chances of ranking within the first three pages of a search engine with a keyword phrase. The more popular the keyword phrases are and the less competition they have, the better your chances of ranking on the top three pages. The KRI is a number or fraction that is the chance of ranking for the chosen keyword. KRI numbers can range from .01 to 5 or more. A KRI number less than .15 is highly unlikely to be able to rank on the Top 30 positions even with optimization.

**KEYWORD RESEARCH** – the process used in search engine optimization that searches for words that are related to a website and or web pages and then performs a discovery process that analyzes which ones yield the highest volume and can bring in the most quality traffic to a website or web page.

**KEYWORD STEMMING** – a process that returns to the root of a word and builds additional words by adding a prefix, suffix, or using a plural of the word. The word can be expanded in either direction and even consist of the addition of words.

**KEYWORD STUFFING** – the practice of adding an inordinate number of keywords to a web page, Meta tag or elsewhere on the webpage to increase the content for search engine optimization purposes. These extra keywords are a violation of the search engine rules especially if they are hidden from a visitor to the web page but visible to the search engine. This is considered Black Hat SEO and usually results in a website being banned by the search engines.

**KEYWORD SUBMISSION** – this is associated with submission of keywords within a pay per click search engine optimization campaign. Keyword submission provides direct short-term results. In a PPC campaign, the advertiser only pays for visitors clicking on keywords not impressions of the keywords.

**KINDLE** – a computer appliance (electronic book) launched in November 2007 and sold by Amazon.com.

**KPIs** - (**K**ey **P**erformance **I**ndicators) the keyword phrases that best describe the purpose or focus of the website and help categorize what products or services characterize your offerings to the search engines. These KPIs are used in a Search Engine Optimization program to gain the highest visibility in the search engines to promote visitors to a website.

# L

**LANDING PAGE** – the page where visitors arrive after clicking through a search and landing on a website. The landing page is critical in SEO and paid search because its focus is that of the keyword or keyword phrase entered. The more the landing page focuses on the keyword entered, the more the visitor will be apt to positively respond to the call to action.

**LATENT SEMANTIC INDEXING** – Commonly abbreviated as LSI. This is an algorithm used by Google to determine how words are related to each other in the context of a web page. An article about "*chocolate*" might contain words such as milk, cocoa, boiling, or heating for example.

**LEAD GENERATION** – a visitor to a website who fills out a contact form or downloads a white paper in order to obtain more information about a company, their products, or services.

**LINK BAITING** – the process of encouraging links from other web sites by offering free content, advertisement on a website, widgets, or other enticements of value to them to make external websites or blogs, newsletters, etc. connect to a website. This will result in a positive increase in rank for that web site. This is a common activity in Search Engine Optimization.

**LINK CHECKER** – any number of tools used for checking for broken hyperlinks on a website or web page.

**LINKEDIN** – a business oriented social networking website, started in December 2002, setup to strengthen professional and business contacts. Linkedin.com allows registered users to create and maintain a list of contacts of people they know and trust to gain introductions to others, list job openings and consulting opportunities, or to get references from people that will help them in their business life.

**LINK FARMS** – the practice of purchasing links for a website from an online organization that are usually irrelevant to the focus of that website. The primary purpose of purchasing irrelevant links is to increase the ranking of a website. In Search Engine Optimization, the increase of links from search engines can increase a website's ranking. But, if those links are not relevant to the website or web pages then the website is accused of unethical practice which can result in the website being penalized or banned by the search engines.

**LINK POPULARITY** – a numeric value representing the number of websites linking to a particular website. Link Popularity is an important factor in Search Engine Optimization because website ranking is directly tied to the number of links to a website – the greater the number of links the higher a website will be ranked.

**LINKS** – text that appears highlighted when a user clicks on it and that then takes the user from one location, usually a web page or content, to another destination.

**NOTE:** Search Engine Optimization values links from high quality sources (PR values of 4 or higher) will increase a website's ranking, while links from websites that are not relevant to a site's keywords (PR values of 0, 1 or 2) will decrease a ranking.

**LINK TEXT** – the text that is contained within a link.

**LINUX** – an open source version of the UNIX operating system that is available at no charge over the Internet.

**LOG FILE** – is a file of a website's activity that is recorded on a web server.

**LOG-IN** – the process of gaining access to a website's whitepapers, software programs, or downloading documents that are restricted to all except registered visitors. Logging-in requires a visitor to type in a username, also referred to as a screen name or nickname, and password. A log-in is used to attribute visits, downloads, or requests, etc. to unique users and to track users.

**LOGO** – a graphical symbol, emblem, or icon that acts as a trademark or identifier of a company or brand.

**LONG TAIL KEYWORD PHRASE** – a term used in Search Engine Optimization or Pay-per-Click that was first popularized when Chris Anderson used it in a Wired Magazine 2004 article. It refers to a keyword phrase that consists of more than a single keyword, in most cases three or four keywords, in order to take it from general terms to be more specific to a website. In either manner the results are more visitors to answer a call to action and increase website conversions.

**LOW KEY FOCUS ELEMENTS** - refers to the lesser elements on a web page that are used to optimize a web page.

Low key focus elements include, Meta keyword tags, Meta description tags, Alt tags, link text, bold text, and Italic text.

**LOYALTY PROGRAM** - a marketing program that recognizes and rewards customers based on their purchasing behavior.

**LURKER** – an individual who reads certain blog entries but never participates in them or otherwise indicates his presence.

**LYCOS** - a search engine, launched in 1994, that ceased operations with respect to crawling the web to index in its database in April 1999. Lycos.com only provides access to human-powered results from LookSmart for queries and crawler-based results from Yahoo for other search engines.

# M

**MARKETING ANALYTICS** – a tracking system that works by installing a JavaScript tracking code on each web page from which one requires data. The system then tracks the behavior of visitors to the website. Most analytics measure factors such as visitor page views, visitors to the website, sources of traffic, bounce rate, visitors arriving at specific landing pages, new and returning visitors, keywords, and conversion statistics from visitor to buyers for a website. Through the use of analytics one can fine tune a marketing campaign.

**MAXIMUM BID** – in a cost per click (CPC) campaign, this is the highest amount an advertiser is willing to pay for a visitor to click on their keyword phrase (ad).

**MEMBERSHIP** – refers to belonging to a group. Social networking offers similar benefits of group membership, without the need for as much face-to-face meeting.

**META DESCRIPTION TAG** – HTML code that has a brief description of the web page it is included on. The purpose of the Meta description is to give the search engines a description of the web page.

**META KEYWORD TAG** - HTML code that has a set of key terms or phrases that describe the web page it is included on.

**META TAG** – the HTML code that represents the title, description, and keywords of the content of a webpage that provides a summary of that page's content for a search engine. Black Hat techniques (SPAM) usually stuff keywords into the Meta tags in order to increase their rankings on search engines.

Keyword Meta Tags lost some of their value in Search Engine Optimization. Title and Description Meta tags are useful to display information about a webpage in the search engine results page and also increase the content for optimization.

**META TITLE TAG** – HTML code that describes the title of a web page, similar to a book title that is included on a title page.

**METRIC** – the collections of data around a visitor's activities or actions. These metrics are used to evaluate online marketing effectiveness.

**MICROSOFT CORPORATION** – a Redmond, Washington based company that was founded by Bill Gates and Paul Allen that is known for its Windows Operating Systems, Internet Explorer, Microsoft Office Suite, and SQL server database among many other software applications.

**MINIMUM BID** – the lowest amount that an advertiser can bid for a keyword phrase and still have the keyword actively show on a paid campaign or an advertiser network. Search engines set the minimum bid for any keyword phrase with amounts ranging from $.05 to $60.

**MIRRORING** – the act of creating multiple copies of websites and web pages on different servers usually with different domain names and registering those copies with the search engines. The copies are treated as SPAM because they increase the relevancy of the web pages artificially and illegally. When search engines discover this practice, they can ban the website.

**MISTER-WONG** - is a large European social networking startup website begun in 2006 in Germany by Kai Tietjen. It is similar to Del.icio.us.com and is available in six languages including English and German.

**MIXX** – a general social and news site which has a category for all types of news. Topics covered include business, entertainment, sports, health and tech. Mixx.com has the ability to create groups to share news with other users.

**MMS** – (**M**ultimedia **M**essaging **S**ervice) a service that offers mobile users all types of products including, ring tones, jokes, video clips, and more over their mobile device.

**MOBLOG** – (**Mo**bile we**B LOG**) a weblog that is a publically accessible personal journal from an individual. A moblog is a blog whose posting originates from a mobile device such as a phone.

**MONETIZE** – to make money from a website from selling products, services, or through the use of advertising that leverages the website traffic, or by implementing a paid search campaign.

**MOUSE OVER** – normally used to see textual information on Flash, PDFs, and other non text producing items. To find out if a particular flash image has an Alt tag, mouse over the image and see if text appears.

**MOVE PERMANENTLY or 301 REDIRECT** – a code that indicates that a website has been moved to a new location.  A 301 redirect, as it commonly referred to, is the preferred method of redirecting websites and web pages to a new location. The length of time to accomplish this is minutes while the effect takes anywhere from a few days to a month for the redirect to be picked up.

**MP3** - (**MP**EG layer **3**) a compressed audio or music format. Its design makes it ideal for downloading these types of files over the Internet.

**MPEG** - an audio compression format that allows almost CD-quality fidelity with only a fraction of the file size by discarding frequencies that cannot be heard by the human ear.

**MSN** – (**M**icro**S**oft **N**etwork) Microsoft, Inc. offers the MSN website, www.msn.com, as a search engine website with a home page that contains news and information.

**MYSPACE** – a social networking website that offers an interaction between friends and a variety of other media such as friend's blogs, groups, photos, music, video, and other more. Myspace.com promotes that type of interaction and networking online.

**MULTIMEDIA** – a presentation that incorporates varied types of media such as text, animated, graphics, video, or music.

# N

**NATURAL LISTING or Natural Search Listing** – the process of achieving a position (rank) without paying or bidding for this listing, naturally or free. The position is achieved based on the search engine's own internal algorithm.

**NATURAL SEARCH ENGINE OPTIMIZATION** – achieving desired visibility (positioning) for a website without bidding or paying for it. Natural Search Engine Optimization occupies about 80% of the search. Pay-per-Click has the other 20%. Most Search Optimization techniques employ a best practice process, proven techniques that yield desired results that include focused copywriting, keywords discovery, Meta tags, and link building.

**NAVIGATION (BAR)** – a set of links at the top, bottom, or sides of a web page that assist in moving from one web page to another throughout a website.

**NEGATIVE MATCH** – negative keyword phrases or phrases used in Google's Pay-per-Click campaign or other paid campaigns to prevent irrelevant click-through charges.

**NETIQUETTE – (Net**work Et**iquette)** a code of conduct for acceptable online behavior for users on the Internet.

**NETSCAPE** – a web browser originally published by Netscape Communications Corporation now a part of AOL, which was once the dominant web browser application. It is still being used today mostly by programmers after its code base was turned over to the Mozilla foundation.

**NEWSCLOUD** – is a social site that focuses on news topics. It is similar to Newsvine.com; each user has a blog and can publish content to be voted up by other users.

**NEWSGROUP** – a public forum website or discussion area that has a moderator. Members can view all the messages posted on the forum and network with others with similar common interests. Example of newsgroups include: www, and www.groups.google.com.

**NEWSREADER** – client software loaded on a computer that has web applications which collect (aggregate) syndicated web content such as news headlines, blogs, and podcasts into a single location for easy viewing.

**NEWSVINE** – an open source, community based website service that allows its members to customize the news viewed on its website by members that have posted articles themselves or posting for others to view and rate.

**NICHE MARKET** – a small targeted group of buyers sharing a common buying habit. Because the market is small, general purpose advertising techniques may not appeal to them and as such they must have their advertising targeted and specific to their interests.

**NO FOLLOW COMMAND** - an HTML attribute, similar to a Meta tag, which instructs search engines not to follow a hyperlink to a web page or be influenced in ranking by that link. Originally, a no follow command was used to combat SPAM; this command is no longer widely used.

**NOT IMPLEMENTED** – the server's response when it does not recognize a request or is not capable of supporting it. There can be many reasons for the server's action but the result is that nothing happens and that is when the warning message is issued.

# O

**OFFLINE** – a term used to refer to a user's computer connection to the Internet. Offline states that the Internet is not available, or there is not a connection established.

**OFFLINE PROMOTIONS** – refers to any promotion of a company or an entity that is not conducted online. Typical offline promotions may consist of having a website printed on business cards, stationary, signage, etc.

**OFF-SITE SEO or OFF-SITE OPTIMIZATION** – refers to the optimization techniques employed in Search Engine Optimization that are carried out **outside** to the website. These tasks include the building of links from relevant third-party websites and blogs, submissions to third-party directions, and content syndication via social media.

**ONLINE** - a term used in online marketing to indicate that there is a connection to the Internet. Being online is the normal way to enter content for blogs and social networks.

**ONLINE COMMUNITIES** - groups of people with shared interests who communicate mainly on the Internet through emails, forums, or other media.

**ONLINE MARKETING** – any advertising that is carried on through the Internet or e-mail.

**ONLINE PRESS RELEASE** – a statement or news release distributed over the Internet. The intended audience is any news websites, news aggregator, or entities for the purpose of announcing a new product, service, or event.

**ONLINE WORLD** – referring to any mix of advertising, searching for goods or services, and everything else associated with being on the web.

**ONSITE SEARCH** – a search that is limited to information residing on a website or webpage. Its main purpose is to find specific products on a website through the use of keyword queries.

**ON-SITE SEO** or **ON-SITE OPTIMIZATION** - optimization tasks that are performed in accordance with Search Engine Optimization techniques that are carried out on the website to make sure that the website can be easily indexed by Search Engines. This is usually a one-time task and is the basis for Search Engine Optimization's foundation. These tasks include website usability design navigations, Meta tags, keyword density and assurance of no broken links.

**OPEN PROJECT DIRECTORY** – Often referred to as DMOZ. DMOZ was derived from d**i**rectory.**moz**illa.org. It was created in 1998 in response to problems getting listed in Yahoo! Directory. DMOZ is a comprehensive, human-reviewed directory of the websites maintained by volunteer editors who access web sites for quality and content. DMOZ editors have the ability to accept or deny a listing to a category in the DMOZ directory.

**OPEN SOURCE SOFTWARE** – any computer software, created in a public collaborative manner,  that allows its source code to be changed, improved, and redistributed in its modified or unmodified form by the user and then to be freely shared and re-distributed.

**OPINION POLL** – surveying a section of the population to gather their views on a specific topic.

**OPR** – (**O**nline **P**ress **R**elease) a statement or news release distributed over the Internet. The intended audience is any news websites, news aggregator, or entities for the purpose of announcing a new product, service, or event.

**OPTIMIZATION** – a series of procedures designed to improve the rank, relevancy of keyword phrases, websites and web pages. These techniques can consist of site redesign, web page content, Meta Title tags, Meta description tags, Alt tags, and more.

**OPT-IN** – a way to obtain the user's permission so that future promotional material can be send to them. This promotion material can consists of email, newsletters, etc.   Unlike SPAM, opt-in requires a user's consent to continue receiving promotional material.

**ORGANIC LISTINGS** – any results that appear in a search engine's result page because of adding keyword phrases and optimization (focusing of a topic) on a website without paying any money to the search engine.

**ORGANIC SEARCH** – is the process of a company's website being found in search at no cost to the company.

**ORGANIC SEARCH OPTIMIZATION (SEO)** – the results that come up naturally (not paid) based on web pages or websites being indexing within a database of a search engine.

The important factor in organic search is discovery of keyword phrases, optimizing web page content, adding Meta and Alt tags, and building external links.

**ORPHAN PAGE** – pages that a website visitor can't get to.

**OUTBOUND LINK** – links from a website to another website or web page regardless of the destination.

**OVERSUBMISSION** – the act of submitting a website to a directory more than once in order to speed up the process of listing a website. If done too many times for no good reason, it will ban a website from being listed.

**OVERTURE** – originally Overature.com was a Pay-per-Click advertising campaign tool offered by Yahoo.com. It was renamed in 2005, and is now called Yahoo! Search Marketing.

# P

**PAGE RANK (GOOGLE)** - the Google technology, often referred to as PR, developed at Stanford University, for placing importance on web pages and websites. At one point, Page Rank was a major factor in rankings of keyword phrases. It has evolved to be just one of the metrics search engines factor into the algorithm that determines a webpage or website's rankings. Google Page Rank is a number from 0-10 (10 being the best). This represents Google's perception of the credibility, authority, and quality of a website.

**PAGE VIEWS** – the number of web pages a visitor has viewed.

**PAGES/VISIT** – the average number of pages a visitor viewed while on a website over a predetermined period of time.

**PAID INCLUSION** –an exchange in which a website owner pays to have web pages or the entire website immediately indexed into a search engine's database. This is done because sometimes a new website may take months to be included in a search engine index. Large websites can ignore this because they are being reviewed and indexed once a month regardless.

**PAID LINK BUILDING** – a practice in which websites are willing to link back to another site for a fee in order to boost that site's rankings or relevancy in the search engines. (See link building)

**PAID LISTINGS** – a directory listing where the advertiser pays the publication to be listed.

**PAID PLACEMENT** – any search results program where the order of a listing's appearance depends on payment made to the search site.

**PAID SEARCH CAMPAIGN** – is a method of placing online advertisements.

**PASSWORD** – a sequence of characters (typically 6 - 8 characters in length), known only to the user, either assigned or created by a user. A password is used to obtain access to a computer network, social website, whitepaper, file, etc.

**PAY-PER-CLICK (PPC)** – a paid advertising method of advertising, banner ads or paid search engine listings, in which the advertisers bid for the position they want in the search results page and set up a monthly limit on spend budgets. The advertiser then pays the latest bid price based on the number of times a visitor clicks through to their website rather than impressions or other criteria.

**PEER-TO-PEER** - the direct interaction between two people in a network. In that network, each peer will be connected to other peers opening the opportunity for further sharing, learning or other communication.

**PERFORMANCE** – referring to how a website responds over a particular period of time.

**PERMANENT REDIRECT** - is a method of redirecting an old web page, website, or link to a new location. In other words, used to display another web page for the web address that a user is trying to visit. A permanent redirect, or called a 301 redirect implies that the move is permanent as opposed to temporary.

**PERSONA** – the establishment of a people category that shares several attributes such as gender, age, location, household income, vacation frequency, marital status, and more. Personas are used to determine the type of person that would be the perfect candidate to search for a given product or service. In this way, products or services can match up ad messages and keyword phrases with the specific people that are likely to be interested.

**PHP** - (**H**ypertext **P**reprocessor) a programming language that enables web developers to create dynamic content that interacts with databases.

**PING** – (**P**ocket **I**nternet **G**rouper) an automatic notification sent when a blog has been updated. It also is a means of indentifying that a computer or server is in communications with one another.

**PINGOMATIC.com** – a blog that updates several websites and blogs by filling out a simple form. Pingomatic.com then pings each blog listed.

**PIXEL** – an individual dot that comprises a graphic image. For example, a 480 by 60 display ad is 480 pixels wide and 60 pixels high.

**PLATFORM** - a framework or system within a media framework. A platform can be mobile telephony or a piece of software that has different modules. These modules can include blogs, forums, and wikis.

**PLAXO** – an online address book and social networking service, founded by Sean Parker (Napster) and Minh Nguyen and other Stanford students, that automatically updates users contact information. All user data is stored on Plaxo.com servers.

**PLUGIN** – a software program that extends the original capabilities of an Internet browser. Some plug-ins can play music, movies, or other browser capabilities. Common plug-ins includes Adobe Acrobat, Apple QuickTime Player, and Adobe Flash.

**PODCAST** - low-cost syndicated digital audio files that are created in MP3 format. A podcast is an audio mini-program broadcast over the Internet. Apple Computer's iPods were the first devices to run podcasts, hence the name podcasts.

**POPULARITY** – a website that is sought after by visitors on the Internet.

**POPUP** - ads that appear over the current windows.

**PORTAL** – a website that is a starting point (gateway) that contains links to many other websites. For example, Yahoo.com, Netscape.com, Altavista.com, and MSN.com are examples of portals that, when entered, can link to other websites that provide services, products, etc.

**POSITION -** where a listing appears in search results based on how relevant that keyword is to the information a search engine has stored in its index. Relevancy is measured from the first position and decreases to the least relative relationship. All search engine results pages (SERP) display 10 listing per page, therefore, the 18th listing would appear on the second page at position number eight. The visibility of keyword phrases drops to zero after the 30th position.

**POP-UNDER AD** – an ad that is visible when a window is closed.

**POST** – the act of entering comment, blog entry, or an opinion online.

**PPC** – a paid method of advertising, banner ads or paid search engine listings, in which the advertisers bid for the position they want in the search results page and set up a monthly or limit spend budget. The advertiser then pays the latest bid price based on the number of times a visitor clicks through to their website rather than impressions or other criteria. (See also Pay-per-Click).

**PRECISION** – a term used in Search Engine Optimization that measures the degree to which a search engine's list of documents matches a query. The greater the number of matching documents listed, the higher the precision. For example, if a search engine lists 100 documents that are found to match a query but only 40 of them contain the searched keywords, then the precision is 40%.

**PR NEWSWIRE -** a web based news and information distribution service for professional communications.

**PRESS RELEASE** – company issued statements released to the media and social sites for distribution. Press releases are not ads but newsworthy stories. Their purpose is to promote a business, service, announcements, or news that benefit the population at large or announce some new or innovative product.

**PROFILE** - the basic information and photo that one provides when signing up for any type of online service. Some social networks require information about what the user is looking for in the service as well as that person's educational background, etc. This information helps members connect because they have common interests and backgrounds.

**PROGRESSIVE SYSTEMS** – a Boston based SEO and SMO service provider. For more information contact us at onlinemarketingterms@gmail.com.

**PROPELLER** – a social news networking site that covers all topics from technology to home decorating. Propeller.com is associated with Netscape.

**PROSPECT(s)** – a visitor that is a potential buyer of goods or services.

# Q

**QUALITY SCORE** – an algorithm associated with Google's ™ AdWords campaign and content network that assigns a numeric value to an advertisement. The Quality Score is determined by factors like the use of keyword phrases in ads, relevancy to people searching for that keyword phrase, landing page containing the keyword phrase, and other Google secret factors that allow a keyword phrase to obtain a higher rank in search engine results. The highest Quality score an ad can obtain is 10.

**QUANTCAST** – a website that views statistics of other websites for the purpose analyzing these sites and reporting quantitive data.

**QUERY** – the word or phrases entered into a search engine's search box (query box) which begins a search for the keyword phrase and ends with the results displayed on a Search Engine Results Page (SERP).

# R

**RANK (RANKING)** - the position (from 1-10) or where a listing appears in the search results page SERP relative to the first listing on that page. In delivering results at the rate of 10 results per page, a search result with the rank of 40 would appear on page four as the last listing (position 10) on that page.

**RECIPROCAL LINK** – a case in which two sites link to and from each other on a website or web page. These links are exchanged through an agreement between the websites.

**REDDIT** - a social network website that covers a wide range of news topics. Reddit.com allows users to post content on its website and then members can vote the posting up in rank according to the number of votes it receives.

**REDIRECT** – a method to redirect a visitor from one website to another. Usually this helps to redirect visitors from an older website to a newer one. **Note:** A 301 redirect implies that the move is permanent as opposed to temporary.

**REGISTER** - the process of providing a username, password and other details when a user wants to access a website that has restricted access. See logging in.

**RELEVANT (RELEVANCY)** – the extent to which visitors to a website or web page are interested in what is offered on the website or web pages. Most search engines value a website and keywords if they match each other.

**REPEAT VISITOR** – a website visitor who returns to a website or web page more than once over a specific time period.

**REPURPOSE** – the process of taking content from one source and reusing it in another format or another purpose on a different source. For example, articles with images can be repurposed and turned into a report or a take away source.

**RESULTS PAGE (SERP)** – the search engine's page that displays the results of a query. The Search Engine Results Page ranks websites from 1 to 10 on each page.

**ROBOT (SPIDER, CRAWLER, or BOT)** – a program of a search engine that compiles listings of websites or web pages by automatically following (crawling) links to the website. Once it lands on a website it copies all the web pages found and stores this information into its index (database) unless it is instructed otherwise by a robot tag.

**ROBOT TAG** – tells a search engine crawler, robot, or bot not to crawl or to crawl a link found by a search engine.

**ROI** – (**R**eturn **o**n **I**nvestment) the amount of money one makes on an ad compared to the amount of money one spends on the advertisement. For example, if one spends $100 on PPC ads and makes $150 from those ads, then the ROI would be 50%. (Calculated as: ($150 - $100) / 100 = $50 / 100 = 50%)

**ROOT DIRECTORY** - the first (top most) directory in a hieratical website structure. The root directory is often referred to as a home page.

**RSS (RSS FEED)** - (**R**ich **S**ite **S**ummary or **R**eal **S**imple **S**yndication) a family of web feed formats that leverage XML for distributing and sharing headlines and information from other web content. RSS is commonly called syndication.

**RSS AGGREGATORS** – software that uses a web feed to retrieve syndicated web content such as blogs, podcasts, and mainstream mass media websites for the purpose of simplifying searching the web for articles. RSS aggregators put all this information on a selected topic in one place to save time.

**RYZE** – a free and a paid social network that connects business professionals and entrepreneurs together.

# S

**SAFARI** – a web browser by Apple, Inc.

**SCRAPING THE COMPETITION** – the practice of obtaining information about a competitor's website by using web tools. Information can include keyword phrases, links, and more. First used by Gary E. Haffer in 2001 in a seminar on Search Engine Optimization.

**SCRIPT**– a programming language that directs a software application to perform specific tasks in a specific order. Most web applications today are written in Java or .Net and not a scripting language.

**SEARCH CRITERIA** – a manner in which a search engine stores web pages according to categories in its database (index).

**SEARCH DIRECTORY** – a compilation of databases of websites. A directory does not use crawlers in order to obtain entries in its search database. Instead, it relies on user interaction and submissions for the content it contains. Submissions are categorized by topic and normally alphabetized, so that the results of any search will start with website descriptions that begin with some number or non-letter character, and then move from A-to-Z.

**SEARCH ENGINE(s)** – a web site that gathers information about websites, web pages, and other sources on the Internet. A search engine stores that information in its internal database. To retrieve information from a search engine the user makes a query using the most relevant keyword phrases they can think of. These keyword phrases are then compared against the categories held in the search engine's database at the time of search. If the search engine's database has information about that topic it displays the information on its results page (SERP) positioning the most relevant information closest to the top of the results and ranking all results in order of importance from one to ten on each page. Depending on the query, this process can occupy several hundred pages to display all the information from the search engine's database.

**SEARCH ENGINE FRIENDLY** – a web page or website is said to be search engine friendly or optimized, focused on a given topic, and set up for ease of navigation if its content and keywords are focused on the website's product or service offering. Websites or web pages that are optimized for search engine crawlers are described as search engine friendly websites.

**SEARCH ENGINE INDEX** – the manner that a search engine stores information about a web page in its database (index).

**SEARCH ENGINE OPTIMIZATION (SEO)** – the process of improving a web site's traffic and visibility through the process of choosing targeted and relevant keyword phrases that are related to a website's product or service offering. These keyword phrases, because of their relevancy to a website, drive traffic to that website. Focusing these keyword phrases on the website's offering along with relating the content, adding Meta Tags and links is commonly known as Search Engine Optimization or abbreviated SEO.

**SEARCH ENGINE RANK** – a number assigned to a keyword phrase indicating the relevance to the category in a search engine database (index). Search engine results (rank) range from one to ten positions in relevance order for each page for both Organic and Paid search results (some pages may not have paid campaigns). This is continued for as many pages of web pages that a search engine has in its database.

**SEARCH ENGINE RESULTS PAGE (SERP)** - the page displayed by the search engine with the results of a search. This page is the listing of web pages where the results of both paid ads and the organic (natural) listings are displayed in order of their relevance to the keyword phrase entered for the query in the search engine's database. This relevance determined by the search engine according to its own standards. There are ten positions for every organic and paid listing on each page of the SERP results.

**SEARCH ENGINE SATURATION** - a term relating to the number of URLs included from a specific web site in any given search engine. The higher the saturation level or number of pages indexed into a search engine, the higher the potential traffic levels and rankings.

**SEARCH ENGINE SPIDER** – a robot, bot, spider, or crawler that follows all links on a website unless told otherwise so that they can be indexed by a search engine.

**SEARCHING (SEARCH)** - normally means to be looking through the Internet with a search engine for information on particular topics. Searchers can look for information on websites, blogs, social sites, wikis, and other locations on the Internet to find information.

**SEARCH QUERY** – a keyword phrase entered into a search engine to obtain information about it.

**SEARCH VOLUME** – is the number of searches, on a search engine, for a keyword phrase in a given month.

**SECOND LIFE** – a social site that is a 3-D virtual world where voice and text are used to communicate, meet others, play online games, and create comic book characters or other likenesses, called avatars, which reflect the users' personalities and behave like them in this virtual online world. The avatars can be directed to act anyway the user wishes them to behave and do anything the user wants them to do.

**SEGMENTATION** – the ability to determine what geographical area is the source of a web site's traffic.

**SEM** –(**S**earch **E**ngine **M**arketing) any marketing activity involving a search site, including advertising on search result pages, paying for placement (Pay-per-Click), and Search Engine Optimization that is used to improve a website's rank and visibility. Search engine marketing is either a pay-per-click campaign (paying for position) or a free campaign called organic or natural search. SEM is often referred to as website marketing, internet marketing or online marketing.

**SEMPO** – (**S**earch **E**ngine **M**arketing **P**rofessional **O**rganization) a nonprofit organization promoting awareness and interest in search engine marketing.

**SEO** –(**S**earch **E**ngine **O**ptimization) the process of improving a web site's traffic and visibility through the process of choosing targeted and relevant keyword phrases that are related to a website's product or service offering. These keyword phrases, because of their relevancy to a website, drive traffic to that website. Focusing these keyword phrases on the website's offering along with relating the content, adding Meta Tags and links is commonly known as Search Engine Optimization or abbreviated SEO.

**SERP** – (**S**earch **E**ngine **R**esults **P**age.) the page displayed by the search engine with the results of a search. This page is the listing of web pages where the results of both paid ads and the organic (natural) listings are displayed in order of their relevance to the keyword phrase entered for the query in the search engine's database.  This relevance determined by the search engine according to its own standards. There are ten positions for every organic and paid listing on each page of the SERP results.

**SHARING** - offering other people the use of your text, images, video, bookmarks or other content by adding tags, and applying copyright licenses that encourage use of content.

**SHOPPING.COM** – a website that features comparison shopping for products and prides itself as delivering discounts for these products. Shopping.com was purchased in August 2005 by eBay.com.

**SHOPPING CART** – a software application that resides on a website which allows for the selection of multiple items and the payment for the items to be made in a single financial transaction.  It is analogous to shopping in a grocery store, where items are chosen and placed in a "shopping cart" for purchase either immediately or at a time when the selection process has been finalized.

**SHOPPING SEARCH ENGINE** – a search engine which specializes in delivering product prices and comparative prices for commonly sought after items.

**SIDEBAR** - single or multiple columns that reside along either or both sides of a blog site's main content area. The sidebar may include contact information of the author, the blog's purpose and categories, links to archives, testimonials, white papers, and other widgets that are included on the site.

**SIGNATURE FILE** – a text file or embedded text associated with an email message that may contain information such as the sender's name, company name, email address, website, and other information that identifies the sender.

**SITE MAP**- a listing one web page of a website that contains all the links that connect a visitor to various parts of the website.  A sitemap is a roadmap of a website and helps visitors to navigate the site.  It also helps search engines crawl through a website to index pages.

**SITE USABILITY** – refers to an evaluation of the components of a usable website. This takes into account navigation, legibility, information organization, getting to the call to action, and other factors that make a website or web page as usable.

**SK*RT** - a general news social website that has a strong female user base.  Its focus is on fashion, entertainment and design.  It also includes other topics like technology and food.

**SKYPE** – low cost software that runs over the Internet with a computer phone and a computer connection. Skype is used for making low cost calls to anyone else who also uses Skype. It can make calls to traditional telephone numbers, receive calls from traditional phones, and receive voicemail messages.

**SLD** – (Second Level Domain) a domain that is right below a top-level domain.  For example, if a top level domain is gary.biz, then the second level domain can be gary.biz.co.

**SMM** – (Social Media Marketing) marketing that uses social media websites and blogs for results.

**SMO** – (**S**ocial **M**edia **O**ptimization) the optimization of social press releases, social sites, and other social blogging sites to obtain results.

**SMS** – (**S**hort **M**essaging **S**ervice) the term applied to text messaging on a mobile device.

**SOCIAL BOOKMARKING** – the collaborative equivalent of storing favorites or bookmarks within a web browser. Social bookmarking services such as FURL, del.icio.us and others allow people to store their favorite websites online and share them with others who have similar interests.

**SOCIAL MEDIA** – the term that describes the tools and platforms that are used to publish, converse, and share content online. These tools and platforms include blogs, social websites, podcasts, wikis, and any website used to share any type of information that consists of audio, video, photos, etc.

**SOCIAL MEDIA MARKETING** - the structured method of using social media to create interest and increase brand identity of a product, service, or special promotion.

**SOCIAL MEDIA OPTIMIZATION** – a strategy used to increase the position of posted content on a social website.

**SOCIAL NETWORK** – a web-based social service that provides ways for users to interact with other users by sharing items in order to build online communities of people with like interests. These items can consist of files, blogging, and online forums.

**SOCIAL SITES** – a web based networking group of users, referred to as an online community, whose activities consist of sharing information about specific topics within their community and outside, passing around content, voicing opinions to other members of the community, and communicating thoughts on product and services to its user base and the Internet.

**SPAM** - any search engine marketing method, SEO or Pay-per-Click that a search engine believes is detrimental to its efforts to deliver relevant, quality search results by the manipulation of techniques that violates the search engine's rules of fair play. SPAM's purpose is to achieve higher rankings for a web page or website by any means possible. When SPAM techniques are used on websites or web pages that website is usually banned by the search engine.

**SPHINN** – a social website for interactive marketing. Sphinn.com was designed to allow sharing and finding of news stories, taking part in discussions, discovering events of interest, and networking with other members of Sphinn.com.

**SPIDER (SEARCH ENGINE SPIDER OR CRAWLER)** - small programs that automatically gather data from websites or web pages for a number of reasons. A spider, crawler, or robot follows links on a website for the purpose of making copies of the web pages found. It then stores that data about the website in the search engine's index (database) in order to update it.

**SPLASH PAGE** – the first page seen by a visitor to a web site. It is meant to grab the visitor's attention and usually contains eye catching graphics.

**SPYWARE** – any type of software installed on a computer without the owner's consent or knowledge. The purpose of most spyware is to have advertisements appear for products, services, or other websites to sell their offerings. The threat is also present that spyware will send sensitive information from the computer it has invaded to other locations over the Internet.

**SQUIDOO.COM** – a free social website, a wiki originally created by Seth Godin, that is a network of single pages created by users, referred to as lenses, that focuses on an individual's or company's point of view, recommendations, or expertise on a specific topic.

**STICKINESS** - the length of time a visitor spends at a website during a given visit. If a reader sticks around to view many web pages, then the web pages are considered sticky meaning that the visitor didn't just pop in and leave. This word has been replaced by bounce rate.

**STOP WORD** – words (for example, and, of, the) that can appear in the content on a website or webpage but that have no search value.

**STOVEPIPE** – a vertical line character "|" (called stove pipe) used as a separator for keyword phrases or other category of words in Search Engine or Pay-per-Click campaigns. It is commonly found in Meta Title Tags, Meta Description Tags, Pay-per-Click ad copy, etc.

**STREAM** –the method by which digital content, video or audio, arrives at a computer in a constant flow of information. Streaming requires a significant amount of bandwidth and if a service provider does not have enough bandwidth then the display will start and stop randomly, as opposed to downloading an entire file and then playing it.

**STUMBLEUPON** – a social network and browser toolbar which allows users to discover and rate web pages, websites, photos, video, and news articles. StumbleUpon.com is currently owned by eBay.com.

**STYLE SHEET** – the way the look and feel of a website is determined.

**SYNCHRONOUS COMMUNICATIONS** - communications over the Internet that occur in real time. Examples of real time communications include the chat, audio or video capabilities of some website services. This communication can occur in the same location or in different places.

**SYNDICATION** – the process that allows news, content, or blogs to be distributed online through a broad network of websites.

# T

**TAG(s)** – a keyword phrase attached to online content, bookmark, photo, video or other type of content so that it can be easily found later by searching or feed aggregators.

**TAGGING** – a way of categorizing online content using keywords that describe what can be found at a blog post, website, bookmark or photo.

**TARGET AUDIENCE** – the group of people selected that are most likely to purchase an organization's products or services based on characteristics that are identified such as age, income, location, buyer preferences, etc., based the group's past purchase behavior and demographics.

**TECHNORATI** – an Internet search engine that tracks blogs and other media in real time and posts the finding within minutes of receiving new content.

**TELECONFERENCING** - the process of holding a meeting without being in the same place. Teleconferencing takes place over a network connection and by using tools like Voice over IP (VOIP), Instant Messaging, Video, and Whiteboards.

**TELENET** – an Internet service that allows a remote computer to connect to, log in, a local one for reasons like manipulation or setting up a session.

**TERMS OF SERVICES** - the terms which a user agrees to adhere to in order to use a forum or other web-based place for creating or sharing content.

**THREADS** – the paths of online conversation referring to messages, emails, feedback, or content that relates back to an original message.

**THUMBNAIL** – a smaller version of the full sized image on a web page. The thumbnail usually contains a hyperlink to a full size version of the image.

**TIME PERIOD** – the period of time measurements are taken to determine a website's performance.

**TITLE TAG(S)** - a Meta data element, in HTML code, placed in the code section behind each page on a website that states the title (focus) of any web page.   The title tag appears in the top bar of your browser. It is also the hyperlink that appears in the search engine results listings (SERPs). Title tags are important because it is a way that individuals and search engines can determine the topic of particular web pages.

**Note:** Certain words in the title appear in bold if they match (a measure of relevancy of the searched keyword and the website page) the individual's search query.

**TLD** – (Top Level Domain) the three main domain extensions: .com, .net, .org.

**TOOLBAR** – a graphical user interface that usually consists of either a horizontal row or a vertical column of selectable images or graphical buttons. The toolbar allow the user to select a given web page or other functions.

**TOPIC** - an online discussion idea, issue, or a talking point in a conversation that is made up of threads.

**TOUCH POINTS** – the number of contacts a customer has with a brand and website usually during a sales process or after a sale is made. It is important because the more contact one has with a client the better the chances that repeat sales will be made.

**TRACKBACK** – a blog notification that allows a blog, original author, to see who has seen the original post and has written an entry about it.

**TRAFFIC** – a measurement of the number of visitors to a website usually determined by using a web analytics tool that has embedded code within a website.

**TRAFFIC SOURCES** – the sources of visitors prior to visiting a website.

**TWEET(s)** – a message posted on Twitter that is up to 140 characters long.

**TWITTER** - a free social networking website that is focused on staying in touch with friends, family and co-workers. Twitter allows members to post text messages (Tweets) by the use of mobile text (SMS), instant messaging, and email so that everyone can stay connected and inform others of their activities. Twitter's basic question is "What are you doing?" This requires members to supply a short answer and can lead to collaboration.

# U

**UNIQUE VISITOR** – an individual visitor to a web site tracked by a unique identifiable quality (typically an IP address) by the web site host server in a given time period. If a visitor arrives at a web site 50 times and clicks on links, it is still counted as one unique visit.

**UPGRADE** – the process of installing a newer and more powerful version of a software package, hardware, or a newer version of an existing system.

**UPLOAD** – the process of transferring a file or files (data) from a local computer (usually on its hard disk) to another remote computer usually associated with a website.

**URL** - (**U**niform **R**esource **L**ocator) commonly referred to as a web address.

**USABILITY** – the process of making a website an easy place to move around and locate information in. Factors such as easy to understand menus, relevant content on the web pages, and direct linking to main topics constitutes a website that is easy for a visitor to locate information. Usability also makes it easy for search engine crawlers to navigate through a website for optimization purposes.

**USERNAME** – a unique way to identify a user when that user logs into a computer network, account, a restricted website, etc.

# V

**VERISIGN** – a California company that provides authoritative routing support for every web address ending with .com or .net on the Internet. Estimates show that there are nearly 18 billion domain name queries every day.

**VIEW SOURCE CODE** – the process of looking at the code behind each web page by using the source option on a browser.

**VIRAL MARKETING** – any marketing technique that uses social networks as a low cost alternative to traditional advertising to increase brand awareness to users, or to pass on a marketing message to other websites, users, blogs, or people. Through viral marketing a potentially exponential growth in the message's visibility and effect can be created. A viral campaign is analogous to the spread of computer viruses – once it begins it spreads exponentially in a short time.

**VIRTUAL WORLDS** - online places, like Second Life, where a person can have a representative, an avatar, live in a virtual world and take on any personality to socialize and interact with other members. Basic membership is free and items can be purchased like land, cars, countries, and other accessories with real money.

**VIRUS** – a dangerous computer application that spreads quickly (exponentially) through the opening of emails from user to user or by incorporating into any program on a computer. Viruses are meant to cause damage once they are activated and can corrupt data files, programs, or completely disable a computer's operation.

**VISITOR(s)** – an individual who has viewed a web site or web page.

**VOICE OVER INTERNET PROTOCOL (VOIP)** – enables a computer or other Internet device, best known is Skype, to make local, international, and conference calls for very low rates with no roaming charges. VOIP uses a headphone and a microphone plugged into a USB port on a computer to make calls anywhere for pennies per minute.

# W

**W3C** – (**W**orld **W**ide **W**eb **C**onsortium) the main international standards organization for the Internet. Complying with W3C standards is voluntary, but creating bad links can result in serious penalties from the major Search Engines.

**WAP** – (**W**ireless **A**pplication **P**rotocol) allows users to access information instantly via handheld devices such as mobile phones, pagers, two-way radios, smart phones and other mobile devices.

**WEB 2.0** – a collection of web-based communities, services, and programs with the purpose of collaboration and sharing between users.

**WEB ANALYTICS** – a software application that is used to measure and track a visitor's activity on a website with respect to traffic parameters over a given time period. Web analytics software measures visitors, new visitors, bounce rate, page view, and more.  Analytics usually function by placing a piece of code on the web pages for which data is needed.

**WEB-BASED TOOLS** - any type of tool available today that can be used with search engines.  Search engines like Google, Yahoo, and others provide an increasing range of free or low-cost tools including email, calendars, word processing, and spreadsheets that can be used on the web rather than on a desktop.

**WEB BROWSER** - a software application which allows an Internet user to display and interact with content on a website, web page, or other types of online content.

**WEBCAST** – streaming video or downloaded information that is broadcast over the Internet. A webcast consists of sound or video delivered over the Internet live or delayed. Webcasts typically are used to update news, weather, or other selected information.

**WEBINAR** – (**Web-based seminar**) a presentation, lecture, workshop or seminar that is transmitted over the Web and is unique because of its ability to interact with the audience on a specific topic.

**WEBMASTER** – the designated person who manages a website.

**WEB PAGE** – the interior parts of a website that contains text, graphics, URLs, and hyperlinks to other web pages or external sources. Web pages may also contain video, podcasts, white papers, etc.

**WEB PAGE CODE** – It the code that comprises a website and it is usually in HTML.

**WEBSITE**  - a collection of images, text, audio, graphic, content, and other elements displayed on the individual web pages of a website.

**WEBSITE DESIGN** - the various pages of a website that are connected or linked by URLs that serve to direct the visitor to the next page or jump around to any page. Websites are collections of information about particular topics, products, or services. A web site might be compared to a book, where each page of the book is a web page.

**WEBSITE PERFORMANCE** – is what the website has produced over a specific duration of time.

**WEBSITE SUBMISSION** - the act of supplying a search engine or directory with a URL and a short profile about an organization. This is done in order to make the search engine or directory aware of a website or web page.

**WET PAINT** – a free and easy to use and edit wiki hosting service, established in October 2005, for non-technical people who want to collaborate online with others in a simple way. Wetpaint.com gets revenue from contextual advertising on its websites.

**WHITE HAT SEO** - the use of accepted Search Engine Optimization practices in order to get higher rankings, more traffic, better conversions, and less bounces from a web page.

**WHITEPAPER** – a document that became popular in the late 1990's. It is used as a marketing tool that explores a theme or narrow topic in detail. Whitepapers are usually longer than four pages and some approach twenty-five pages. The purpose of a whitepaper is to educate and help readers make decisions on a company's offerings by revealing the benefits of services, products, or technologies.

**WHOIS** - one of several Internet utilities that supply a variety of information to anyone looking for domain histories, web hosting reports, ownership information of the domain name, and webmasters for a particular website.

**WIDGET** - a term used for a graphical user interface between an application and a operating system.  Widgets display information and allow users to manipulate them for particular results. Typical widgets include calendars, tip calculators, etc.

**WI-FI** – (**Wi**reless **Fi**delity) refers to any types of wireless local networks that allow handheld device like, an Apple iPhone, Blackberry, and etc. connection to the Internet.

**WIKI** - an easy to edit, collaborative website, whose name is taken from the Hawaii language meaning – quickly, quickly. A Wiki collects information on particular topics and allows multiple people online to interact. Wiki's technology is like a blog, but Wikis are simpler to use. Basic functions like editing, deleting or modifying content can be performed by anyone. Wikipedia, an online encyclopedia, is an example of a Wiki.

**WIKIPEDIA** – the largest, multilingual, free, most extensive, web-based encyclopedia currently available on the Internet. Wikipedia.com entries are made by volunteers and the articles encourage collaborative editing by anyone with access to the web and registered with Wikipedia.

**WORDPRESS** – free software that allows its users to create blogs. Wordpress.com is one of the most popular open source blogging software platforms and offers a downloadable blogging program and a hosted solution.

**WORLD WIDE WEB** – was created in Geneva, Switzerland by Sir Tim Berners-Lee in the early 1990s. The reason for its creation was to improve communications among researchers of the time.

**WYSIWYG** – (**W**hat **Y**ou **S**ee **I**s **W**hat **Y**ou **G**et) important in text editing because it is associated with various text editors such as MS Word, Front Page, Dreamweaver and other WYSIWYG editors.

# X

**XENU LINK SLEUTH** – a free software program for checking websites for broken internal or external links and creating a sitemap. In Search Engine Optimization broken links negatively impact website quality.

**XING** – a global social networking platform. Xing.com, founded in August 2003 in Hamburg Germany, was created for professionals to manage their business contacts. It is considered competition to Linkedin.com. Xing has over 6 million business professional members worldwide.

**XML** – (**E**xtensible **M**arkup **L**anguage) a data delivery language that is used to format and structure information.

**XML FEED** – an annual fee that is paid to the search engine or a fee paid on a cost-per-feed basis to make the search engine crawl a website on a regular basis. The web pages of a website are sent to the search engine via a XML format more frequently than waiting for the indexing to occur to update a search engine database.

**XML SITEMAP** – a listing of all links on a website that are in XML language and used by Google to create a Google Sitelink and crawl a website.

# Y

**YAHOO** – an Internet portal company which was started with the popular **Yahoo! Directory** created by David Filo and Jerry Yang. It has been one of the most visited websites on the Internet.

**YAHOO ANSWERS** - a community-driven question asking and answering service, started in December 2005, that was formally called Ask Yahoo!. It is basically a social site that has built up content from its membership. Its closest rival is Google.

**YOUTUBE** – one of the many social video websites where users can upload, view, and share video content like movie videos, video clips, and more. YouTube.com was formed in February of 2005 in San Bruno California by three former PayPal employees and in November 2006 purchased by Google, Inc. for 1.65 billion dollars.

# INDEX

www.ingramcontent.com/pod-product-compliance
Lightning Source LLC
Chambersburg PA
CBHW071424050326
40689CB00010B/1972